MUDDY COWS

MUDDY COWS
by John Godber

JOSEF WEINBERGER PLAYS

LONDON

MUDDY COWS
First published in 2014
by Josef Weinberger Ltd
12-14 Mortimer Street, London W1T 3JJ
www.josef-weinberger.com / plays@jwmail.co.uk

ISBN: 978 0 85676 356 4

Printed by Commercial Colour Press plc, Hainault, Essex

JOHN GODBER

One of the most performed writers in the English language, John Godber was born in Yorkshire in 1956. A trained teacher with an MA in drama, it was whilst teaching from 1981-83 that he gained national recognition, winning major awards at the National Student Drama Festival and Fringe Firsts at the Edinburgh Festival. In 1984 he was appointed artistic director of Hull Truck Theatre Company. He has written over forty stage plays including *Bouncers, September in the Rain, Happy Jack, Up 'n' Under, Blood, Sweat and Tears, Teechers, Salt of the Earth, Cramp, Happy Families, Gym and Tonic, It Started With a Kiss, Passion Killers, Unleashed, Thick as a Brick, April in Paris, Lucky Sods, On the Piste, On a Night Like This, The Office Party, Losing the Plot* and *Muddy Cows*.

With Jane Thornton he has co-written *Shakers* and an adaptation of Bram Stoker's *Dracula*. He has also written extensively for television including *Crown Court, Grange Hill* and *Brookside*, the six part BBC series *The Ritz* and its sequel *The Continental*, the screenplay *My Kingdom For A Horse* and the film of *Up 'n' Under*. John also devised the BBC series *Chalkface*, and has written the sports documentary *Body and Soul* for Channel Four Television.

MUDDY COWS was first presented by the Stephen Joseph Theatre Company at the Stephen Joseph Theatre, Scarborough on 4th July 2013. The cast was as follows:

MAGGIE DEAKIN	Elizabeth Carling
DONNA COOKE	Claire Eden
FRAN WOOD	Una McNulty
AMBER MATTHEWS	Hayley Tamaddon
KIM JOHNSON	Amy Thompson
DAISY COOKE	Claire Eden
JESS BAXTER	Abi Titmuss

Directed by John Godber

Set design by Pip Leckenby

Lighting design by Paul Steer

ACT ONE

Scene One

A field. Night.

A large bag of muddy balls is thrown to one side, a few flags also lay on stage, a number of old tyres are also on stage, as are a few tracksuits and coats. Maggie *runs on stage carrying a tyre in each hand. She wears an old and worn England women's international rugby tracksuit and is wrapped against the weather, she shouts off stage to her team. When the women emerge they are dressed in tracksuits and hoods/beanie hats, which gives their appearance a very masculine feel.*

MAGGIE   Come on, keep it going girls. Come on Donna, Daisy make it work, push it Jess, come on Amber you lazy sod! Go Daisy, move your frame, come on girls, make it count. Fran, push it, come on Jess Baxter push it, keep it going!

                    (JESS *enters, she is carrying a two tyres on in each hand. She throws the tyres to the floor, angry at her effort and breathing heavily.*)

JESS   Oh!

MAGGIE   Well done Jess.

JESS   You cut the corner!

MAGGIE   Who?

JESS   You cut the corner off!

MAGGIE   I never!

JESS   You should lead by example.

MAGGIE   That's what I do to win, Jess, I cheat!

JESS   You'll have to do with this team!

MAGGIE   You call this a team?

JESS   That's what you said it was!

MAGGIE   Hey, I know what's what, I'm not deluding
              anybody, I know where we are, just so you
              know . . .

JESS   Are you sure?

MAGGIE   Hey listen, I've been there!

JESS   I wasn't saying you haven't!

MAGGIE   It's baby steps, mate!

JESS   You should find a better club though Maggie,
              because this is getting ludicrous.

MAGGIE   Oh and that'd make sense wouldn't it?

JESS   I mean there must surely come a point . . .

MAGGIE   Emma started here.

JESS   For one season!

MAGGIE   That's not the point Jess!

JESS   So what is the point?

MAGGIE   This is where she started playing.

JESS   She played for one season, and then the club
              folded, because of lack of interest, you've told
              us that a hundred times! She started here and she
              moved on; that's what happens!

MAGGIE   Oh I'm not getting into this tonight!

JESS   Well there must be easier ways!

MAGGIE   To what?

JESS   Well if you're on a mission!

MAGGIE   Is that supposed to be funny?

JESS   You need to speak to Jack Peel about it.

MAGGIE   I'm blue in the bloody face trying to get a
              meeting with the silly fat sod!

JESS   Oh whatever . . .

MAGGIE   Do you think I don't know that they're laughing
              at me behind my back, that's what makes me
              want to make it bloody well work! It's all about
              access and development if you talk to the board,
              but there's no frigging money for us to develop
              and allow access, so fathom that out! I wasn't
              born yesterday you know, I know where we are!

JESS   Well you need to drop a pebble and get on the
              radar.

MAGGIE   Yes that's right because it's that easy, we're
              struggling to get nine turn out on a regular basis!

JESS   I know that, bloody embarrassing!

MAGGIE   Well what do you suggest I do? It's taken me six
              months to get them to commit to actually training
              . . . they don't have to be here you know?

JESS   You wonder why they do!

MAGGIE   So shall I tell 'em they're never going to make it
              and they're shit, is that what you'd do?

JESS	I'm not running the club Maggie!
MAGGIE	Amen to that darling.
JESS	Absolutely!
MAGGIE	Amen to that!
	(MAGGIE *turns to call to the team, off stage.*)
	Come on Kimbo . . .
JESS	It's just not how you sold it to me.
MAGGIE	Baby steps Jessica . . . they're doing their best!
JESS	Yes that's my point!
MAGGIE	What point?
JESS	They're not really are they . . . you need to raise the bar . . . because this is just treading water of you ask me mate!
MAGGIE	Raise the bar . . . that's good . . . we haven't even got any frigging kit, and you want to raise the bar; hallelujah to that . . . good grief!
	(KIM *enters with a tyre in her hand.*)
KIM	Killing me!
MAGGIE	Well done Kimbo.
KIM	Maggie cut the corner off!
JESS	I know she did.
	(KIM *throws the tyre down and sits in it.* MAGGIE *calls off.*)

Maggie	Come on Fran, come on!
	(Fran *enters slowly with a tyre, but she has it around her neck.*)
	You are supposed to carry it!
Fran	Bollocks to that!
	(Fran *throws the tyre onto the field.*)
Maggie	Well done!
Jess	Well done Fran!
Fran	I couldn't get my breath.
Maggie	No wonder with it round your neck!
Fran	That's why I put it around my neck.
Kim	Maggie cut the corner off!
Fran	(*exhausted*) I could cut my head off!
Kim	I think I've lost a nail.
Jess	Well done you two!
Kim	Couldn't find it.
Jess	You mean you stopped to look for it?
	(Maggie *calls off angrily to* Amber.)
Maggie	Come on Amber, try for once; you should've been the first one back.
	(Amber *enters at a slovenly pace; carrying two tyres.*)

AMBER   What a fiasco!

MAGGIE   You're supposed to run!

AMBER   With two?

MAGGIE   We have.

AMBER   You cut the corner off!

MAGGIE   Why have you got two?

AMBER   Daisy dropped hers because she'd got a call out. A cow's been shot near Filey! I think it's an excuse for her to go early. Donna's coming . . . she'll do Daisy's subs she said.

MAGGIE   I can't tell which one is which.

AMBER   Nobody can!

          (AMBER *gets her breath as* MAGGIE *calls off to* DONNA.)

MAGGIE   Come on Donna keep going!

          (AMBER *puts two tyres together and sits on them. The girls are exhausted.*)

KIM   I lost a nail.

AMBER   I lost the will to live!

          (DONNA *enters carrying a sack of spuds in front of her.*)

DONNA   Oh fucking hell!

          (JESS *applauds, as do the others in a tired fashion.*)

JESS	Well done Donna!
	(DONNA *throws the spuds onto the stage and fights to get her breath.*)
MAGGIE	Where's your tyre?
DONNA	I didn't take a tyre, I don't like the smell. I saw a pile of spuds so I thought . . . Hey did you cut the corner off?
JESS	Yes, she bloody did!
MAGGIE	Don't do as I do, do as I say!
KIM	Do be, do be do . . .
	(*The girls are exhausted, and they variously pant, squat and get their breath back. There is much hugging and support for each other.*)
AMBER	Did you see those two in that car?
JESS	I saw them.
AMBER	Were they dogging?
JESS	Well they weren't snogging!
FRAN	Perverts!
DONNA	I felt like a pervert watching 'em.
JESS	No wonder if you were just stood there holding your spuds!
FRAN	So to speak!
AMBER	They probably thought we were the perverts running around with tyres!

DONNA   Like a cult?

FRAN   I felt like a cult cutting through the caravan park.

               (*The girls laugh at this near miss.* MAGGIE *re-addresses her troops.*)

MAGGIE   Okay girls grab your tyres, let's push out ten presses, we'll skip the tyre flipping tonight. Here we go . . . Ready, come on.

ALL   Oh what? Mag!

MAGGIE   Nice good ones. Come on and, one, two, three, four, five, six, seven, eight, nine, ten!

               (*They perform the exercises with varying degrees of aplomb.*)

               And put them down, now curls for ten, come on, keep it going – one, two, three, four, five, six, seven, eight, nine, ten!

               (*They perform the curling exercises with some effort.*)

               Well done, well done ladies! A few line out moves please. Amber grab a ball, let's have a few calls.

               (*The girls know exactly what is required of them.* AMBER *grabs a ball, as* KIM, *plays scrum half,* JESS *plays number ten,* DONNA *and* FRAN *line up with* MAGGIE *between them for a line out.*)

AMBER   Call it!

DONNA   Scarborough Fair three!

               (AMBER *throws the ball high,* DONNA *and* FRAN *lift* MAGGIE *who catches the ball, and* KIM *collects it, she passes it to* Jess *who in turn passes to* Amber *who has run from the line out to play outside centre. The move is done with ease and casual excellence.*)

MAGGIE   Very good. Again!

(The girls casually make their way back to the same positions and they perform the same exercise again, almost in slow motion because they have no opposition, it is so easy for them.)

AMBER   Call it!

DONNA   Harbour bar thirteen!

(This time MAGGIE *is replaced by* FRAN *who taps the ball to* KIM, *and the same movement is played out.* MAGGIE *applauds their efforts.)*

Well done ladies, and now the most painful thing of all. Get your cash out girls, subs time please! Two quid for the pleasure; come on flash the cash. Donna you're paying for Daisy!

DONNA   Am I?

AMBER   That's what she told me.

(MAGGIE *has a small money bag and she collects subs as the girls find their cash in the tracksuits.* MAGGIE *goes to* KIM.)

MAGGIE   Two pounds girls, let's keep this boat afloat, I'll accept a tenner if you've got no change, all donations welcome! Thanks Kimbo.

KIM   Two pounds exactly.

(DONNA *puts her money in the bag.*)

DONNA	That's for me and our Daisy then.
MAGGIE	I thought she had all the money?
DONNA	You know why?
MAGGIE	She never spends any!

(MAGGIE *approaches* AMBER.)

AMBER	Fiver!
MAGGIE	Cheers!
AMBER	No change?
MAGGIE	I'll take it for two weeks.
AMBER	Unfair.
MAGGIE	You missed last week.
JESS	She can't remember that far back.

(MAGGIE *moves to* JESS.)

AMBER	I thought I'd paid it.
FRAN	She did, but that was for the previous two weeks!
JESS	Fiver.
MAGGIE	Every little helps!
JESS	How are we doing?
MAGGIE	Well, we won't be buying a mini bus just yet.
JESS	Can we afford to hire one?
MAGGIE	He says he's putting his costs up!

(MAGGIE *moves to* FRAN, *who puts money in the bag.*)

FRAN   Him and British Gas . . . is there a game this weekend?

MAGGIE   I'll let you know.

FRAN   Let me know if we can get fifteen, I'll put a flag up!

                (MAGGIE *begins to secret the bag in her tracksuit, and calls to her troops.*)

MAGGIE   I'm going to drag somebody off the streets. Can you deposit the training equipment in the facility provided.

AMBER   Do you mean put these tyres in the container?

MAGGIE   That is the facility provided!

                (*The girls begin to pick up a number of tyres and exit with them.*)

AMBER   Are you coming on Wednesday, Fran?

FRAN   To carry you home?

DONNA   I'd better run . . .

AMBER   You coming Donna?

DONNA   Is it posh?

AMBER   We're going round town, you decide.

KIM   I'm off Maggie, Bret's working late and I've got an appointment at the shop. See you Wednesday!

ALL   Cheers!

                     (AMBER *collects a number of tyres, as does*
                     DONNA *with her spuds and a tyre held at arm's*
                     length.)

AMBER   Shall I bung this in the facility provided?

MAGGIE   If you would.

                     (KIM *exits taking some of the tyres with her,*
                     AMBER *also collects her kit bag and a number*
                     of tyres and exits. There is a moment's repose
                     as MAGGIE *and* JESS *get their breath and collect*
                     their thoughts.)

JESS   How come we can't use the scrum machine like
                     the under-seventeens?

MAGGIE   That's one of life mysteries.

JESS   And how come we can't use the gym anymore?

MAGGIE   We can on Wednesdays after half seven, Jack
                     tells me; except Donna feels that they're all
                     talking about her, so. All being well we've got
                     Preston Grasshoppers a week on Sunday if they
                     can get a team.

                     (JESS *begins to collect her kit and some of the*
                     tyres.)

JESS   Better session any way.

MAGGIE   Better than last week, more turned out.

JESS   Touch and pass in the fog?

MAGGIE   Always a challenge!

JESS   Better than being out with the doggers.

Maggie	Maybe the doggers were here last week, but we didn't see them because of the fog?
	(There's an uneasy kinship between these two star players.)
	What's the party for?
Jess	It's Amber's, "just split up" party!
Maggie	Again?
Jess	You know what she's like, she's the only Solicitor I know who actually solicits! We're going round town. Are you coming?
Maggie	The Captain dines alone.
Jess	You always say that, and you always turn out.
Maggie	Curiosity!
	(Jess *starts to collect the tyres, flags and bags.*)
Jess	Do you want a lift?
Maggie	If you could put some of this in the facility provided.
	(The girls collect all the remaining items on stage.)
Jess	At least we've got one.
Maggie	And that took us long enough.
	(Maggie *has a moment where she feels her knee, which is an old war wound.*)
	Oh, this bloody knee!

JESS   Playing up?

MAGGIE   Absolutely killing!

JESS   (*lightly*) A woman of your age; you should take it
                    easy.

                    (JESS *exits.*)

MAGGIE   I do, do. That's why I cut the corner off!

                    (MAGGIE *grabs the balls and a number of tyres,
                    and grabs the flags and awkwardly makes her
                    way off stage towards the large container they
                    have been allowed to use for a lock up. Music
                    plays. Blackout.*)

Scene Two

A street. Night.

KIM *enters, she is dressed inappropriately for the time and place
and she is slightly drunk, she looks back and calls off stage.*

KIM   Come on . . . Amber . . . what're you doing? No
                    come on!

                    (DAISY *enters she too is dressed up and wears a
                    cowboy hat.* DAISY *is* DONNA'S *identical twin but
                    far more country, and they are only told apart by
                    the fact that* DAISY *is the more educated of the
                    two.* AMBER *enters and she has got a blow-up
                    doll tied to her.*)

AMBER   I've just shown that copper my knickers, you
                    should've seen his face, I know him!

DAISY   What's she like?

KIM	Where's Donna gone, Daisy?
DAISY	Had to go home. Dad's got a problem with one of the lambs . . . she's gone to help.
KIM	Does she still live at home?
DAISY	No sign of her moving!
AMBER	I can't tell you apart.
DAISY	That's what identical twins usually means!
AMBER	I know; you're identical but you're different.
DAISY	Thank goodness!
	(*The girls banter is friendly and loving.*)
AMBER	Where's Jess gone now?
KIM	She said she wanted to see the manager.
AMBER	She's not after him is she?
KIM	Only if he's married!
DAISY	Are you married Amber?
AMBER	Yes, to this doll! No; three times at the alter and three refusals. I'm like a race horse.
KIM	And it was you who pulled out wasn't it?
AMBER	Which is a good trick for a woman if you can do it. Anyway I've got my new mate!
	(AMBER *references the doll she has with her.*)
KIM	I think she's had one too many anyway; again!

AMBER   Hey she's a top surgeon, she needs a bloody
             release, like me!

KIM   Is that what it is?

DAISY   She puts people back together, doesn't she, car
             crashes and all that. They reckon she's a genius
             at what she does.

KIM   She's a piece of work, I'll say that for her.

             (AMBER *is anxious for the loo, she animates with
             her doll.*)

AMBER   I need the loo.

DAISY   Again?

KIM   You've only just been!

DAISY   And you went back in there twice because of that
             bloke at the bar.

AMBER   I know but I'm dying.

             (*A beat.*)

DAISY   What did you finish with Dan for anyway?

AMBER   What apart from the fact that he loved himself?

KIM   My mum says all men do that. (*A beat.*) That's
             why she divorced my dad.

             (*They girls are easy with each other.* AMBER *calls
             off stage, she is becoming agitated.*)

AMBER   Come on Jess, what's she's playing at?
             (*Agitated.*) Are we getting down Boleyn's then or
             shall we have one in that Storm bar?

DAISY | There's always Weatherspoon's.

AMBER | Oh Granddad!

DAISY | Don't knock it, my granddad goes there!

AMBER | Exactly . . . oh, she's here.

(JESS *enters – it would be hard to pin her down as a doctor. She has a bottle of Lambrini with her.*)

KIM | Come on!

JESS | Managed to get this.

AMBER | How come?

JESS | I complained about the length of time it took to serve us.

KIM | Lambrini?

AMBER | It's shit.

JESS | We don't have to drink it . . .

AMBER | We do!

JESS | Where are we going?

AMBER | Storm bar and then Boleyn's.

JESS | A club?

AMBER | Why, where do you want to go?

JESS | I haven't been in a club for years.

AMBER | Oh give up . . . at Fran's fortieth we went to one and you couldn't string a sentence together.

JESS	I was on tablets!
AMBER	You were on something.
DAISY	Where's Fran and Maggie?
JESS	Maggie's in the restaurant, recruiting.
AMBER	Shall we leave 'em?
KIM	They won't know where we are going.
DAISY	We don't know where we're going!
AMBER	Storm bar then Boleyn's.
JESS	I haven't been in there for two years.
AMBER	Well I was there last week and it hasn't changed much. (*Calling off stage aggressively.*) Come on Maggie! (*To the girls.*) She might have played for England but can she gossip. (*Calling off once more.*) Come on Maggie you can borrow my blow up doll!
KIM	Hey; if she is recruiting . . .
	(AMBER *plays along with the notion of the doll playing.*)
AMBER	Yes stick it on the wing, pull the plug out and it's off!
	(*They enjoy this.* AMBER *calls off stage once more.*)
	Come on Maggie!
	(AMBER *gives it up as a bad job.*)

Oh bollocks, leave 'em . . . let's get down the Boleyn's.

KIM   I thought we were going to Storm bar?

JESS   Decisions, decisions.

AMBER   Well let's go to Storm bar and then to Boleyn's.

(AMBER *turns and shouts to* MAGGIE *and* FRAN *who are in the distance.*)

We're going to the Storm bar!

DAISY   Did she hear you?

AMBER   I've no idea.

JESS   We could raffle this Lambrini for the club.

AMBER   Oh that'll help; raffling a bottle of Lambrini . . . this frigging doll!

(AMBER *adjusts her doll.*)

DAISY   A nuisance?

AMBER   Yes and never a good word for anybody.

JESS   Disgusting!

AMBER   Yes come on girls . . . I'm dying for a piss.

(AMBER *makes her way off stage, with* KIM, DAISY *and* JESS *reacting gently.*)

DAISY   Her a Solicitor; you wouldn't believe it would you?

JESS   I just hope she never acts for me!

(DAISY *and* JESS *exit chatting.*)

DAISY	And me.
JESS	She's an ambulance chaser.
DAISY	No win no fee?
JESS	Yes, a bit like the team!

(MAGGIE *and* FRAN *saunter onto stage far more casually.*)

FRAN	Have you seen Amber?
MAGGIE	She's barking!
FRAN	Talk about energy!
MAGGIE	I wish she'd put some into training!
FRAN	She needs to take a battery out.

(*A beat.*)

MAGGIE	Where are they going?
FRAN	Amber said she wanted to go to a club.
MAGGIE	Oh . . .
FRAN	What?
MAGGIE	I've got the T shirt!
FRAN	I've got the T shirt, in fact I've got a wardrobe full of that T shirt!
MAGGIE	I'd drift off but I've promised Jess a lift.
FRAN	I'm dropping Amber in Brid if she doesn't pull.

MAGGIE	Glutton!
FRAN	I'm empathetic.
MAGGIE	Oh is that what it is?
FRAN	It's something!
	(*A beat.*)
MAGGIE	Hey, I'll catch you up pet, I promised I'd ring Jay, it was too noisy in there.
FRAN	How's she doing?
MAGGIE	Oh, she's settling in, she's at Leeds Met; didn't get the grades for Loughborough.
FRAN	Quiet now she's gone, I bet?
MAGGIE	Oh don't Fran. Frank's working away a lot of the time, because there's no work where we are and the cost. Unbelievable! I mean I got a grant, not a flaming loan, tough times.
FRAN	Everywhere you look.
MAGGIE	Oh aye, I know that right enough.
	(*A beat.*)
FRAN	Right; I'll go be a wallflower then.
MAGGIE	You might get lucky!
FRAN	It's what we all wished for once!
MAGGIE	Yes but, then again . . . Better the devil you know.

FRAN	I'm not sure about that either!
MAGGIE	See you in a bit.

(FRAN *walks away from* MAGGIE *who watches her go. She is slightly wobbly on her feet.*)

FRAN	Oh these frigging shoes!

(*A beat.*)

MAGGIE	Go for it girl!
FRAN	I'm going for it, but I'm not sure what "it" is.
MAGGIE	Low and hard Fran! Feet, feet, feet!
FRAN	Oh yes, that's the story of my life.
MAGGIE	What is?
FRAN	I'm low and hard.

(MAGGIE *and* FRAN *laugh at each other,* FRAN *exits.* MAGGIE *watches her, grabs her phone and exits.*)

MAGGIE	Go on with you, you're gorgeous!

(*Music. Blackout.*)

Scene Three

A rugby field.

JESS, KIM *and* DONNA *push on a make shift scrum machine. It consists of a pallet on wheels with two large tin drums screwed in at one end and some foam wrapped around it.* AMBER *is stood on the machine as the girls, who are all in their training kit scrum and push the machine onto the stage.*

AMBER	Push, push, push, feet, feet, feet, come on Donna. Feet, feet, feet, come on you lazy sods! What was that?
	(*The girls stop. They are breathless, they stand from the machine.*)
DONNA	Oh for chuff's sake!
AMBER	Come on Donna, this is what we do here, another three.
KIM	You come off and push!
AMBER	I'm on here doing this!
DONNA	Doing what?
AMBER	Shouting like a mad woman!
KIM	We know that.
AMBER	I'm supposed to be Maggie!
JESS	You haven't got the accent, pet.
	(*They girls enjoy their banter.* AMBER *tries* MAGGIE'S *accent.*)
AMBER	Another two runs get down here now pet come on girls, I played for England; that's why I cut corners off. Okay, ten press-ups!
DONNA	Piss off!
KIM	Well said that, girl!
	(FRAN *enters with a ball and a piece of wood from the pallet.*)

FRAN   You're dropping wood all over the shop.

KIM   At least the doggers have gone.

AMBER   Must have scared them off last week!

                (JESS *walks around the field and stretches, she feels unwell.*)

JESS   I don't know about you guys, but I feel a bit rough.

FRAN   Have you been to work?

JESS   I wouldn't go that far, I've been into the hospital!

AMBER   She wrote herself a sick note.

                (*They find this amusing.*)

DONNA   Was it a good night then, our Daisy never said?

AMBER   We went to Storm and then Boleyn's.

FRAN   And where did you get to Amber?

AMBER   I got a lift.

DONNA   Oh yes, who was he?

JESS   He was alright.

AMBER   He was more than alright, actually!

FRAN   I was waiting for you for twenty minutes!

                (MAGGIE *enters. She knows they are lacklustre.*)

MAGGIE   Very good girls. Almost broke sweat!

FRAN   It's dropping to bits Mag.

(Fran *holds up a piece of the pallet.*)

JESS   I thought we were going to use the scrum
              machine?

MAGGIE   Jack said it needs some tlc.

AMBER   So does this!

KIM   Where did you get it from?

MAGGIE   Frank made it.

JESS   I thought he was a master decorator?

MAGGIE   He is, but he's a shit carpenter! That was a
              Sunday afternoon job.

JESS   He should've been on Blue Peter.

              (MAGGIE *gets out her money bag.*)

MAGGIE   Right girls. Subs, I'm afraid.

              (*There is a huge groan from the group.*)

AMBER   Again? We did this last week.

MAGGIE   What's she like eh, she's got a top job and she's
              as tight as . . .

AMBER   I wish I had; there's a girl in our office who
              works as a lap dancer in Leeds who earns more
              than me. She makes a bloody fortune; she's had
              her tits done and everything.

JESS   Oh no!

AMBER   She's twenty three and she's driving an Audi TT!

(MAGGIE *shakes her bag.*)

MAGGIE   Money ladies please, otherwise we're history.

                  (MAGGIE *does the rounds with the money bag.*)

KIM   Did we pay for this?

MAGGIE   We paid for the pallets.

JESS   Good investment then?

MAGGIE   We do what we can.

                  (MAGGIE *collects more cash.*)

DONNA   I could probably bring a cow to push if this
                  doesn't work Mag.

MAGGIE   Yes?

DONNA   I'm serious!

MAGGIE   I know you are Donna, petal, that's what always
                  worries me!

                  (DONNA *picks up a rugby ball and the girls pass
                  easily between themselves.*)

DONNA   Are we doing any touch and pass?

KIM   Not me, I've got a big shop.

MAGGIE   Anymore for anymore? Splash the cash!

                  (*She goes around with her money bag.*)

DONNA   Where are we on Sunday?

MAGGIE   Preston?

AMBER	Time is it?
MAGGIE	Now or Sunday?
AMBER	Sunday.
MAGGIE	The time it is now, will be the same time it will be on Sunday; but if you are enquiring as to when the match kicks off, it's a morning kick off. Money Jess, thanks.

(JESS *puts her subs in the bag.*)

JESS	Always a pleasure.
FRAN	Can you tell she's a teacher?
AMBER	Morning in Preston?
MAGGIE	Preston Grasshopper Ladies, be good if we could get anywhere near fifteen. Donna, make sure your Daisy gets there.
AMBER	Williams Butcher's in town; his daughter plays somebody told me; might I've worth tapping him up for a few quid Maggie.
MAGGIE	The things you have to do eh?
AMBER	Rather you than me. He's got hair coming out of every orifice!
JESS	How do you know?
AMBER	I used to go out with his son.
KIM	Has he got hair coming out of every orifice?
AMBER	Not every one!
JESS	Just a couple.

(They are all passing the ball easily.)

MAGGIE	It's like getting blood out of a stone, fundraising round here!
KIM	Preston ten o'clock kick off?
AMBER	How come we get all the good gigs?
KIM	How are we getting there?
MAGGIE	It's every-man-Jack, Frank's taking me in the van because he's got a job on at his sisters, she wants him to emulsion two bedrooms.
KIM	So we'll have to get there the night before then?
MAGGIE	We've got to take the fixtures we can.
KIM	That'll not go down too well in our house. Bret's got a first team home game.
AMBER	I'll get something booked for us.
KIM	I'll have to dash, I've not been anywhere near a supermarket this week.
DONNA	Can't Bret go?
KIM	Are you joking?
DONNA	No!
KIM	Will somebody text me?
AMBER	I will.
KIM	"Later's" then, okay!

(KIM *exits. There are a few looks, the rugby ball is still being thrown around.*)

DONNA   The touch and pass has had it then?

(*A beat.*)

FRAN   He's got her exactly where he wants her.

AMBER   Sounds interesting!

(*A beat.*)

DONNA   Right, well I'm away then. Said I'd cook for me Mam if we finished early. See you in Preston; will you text me and all Amber?

AMBER   I'll Facebook you.

DONNA   I'm not on Facebook, that's our Daisy.

AMBER   Don't you think you should have a mark or be branded or something? It would make life simpler! I'll text you then.

DONNA   Cheers then. Shall I bring some treats?

FRAN   Now that sounds like a plan!

MAGGIE   Yes, but don't eat them before the game like you did at Hull!

DONNA   I was starving, I'd come straight off a field! See you's . . .

(DONNA *exits,* AMBER *prepares to exit.*)

AMBER   I'll come with you.

FRAN   Probably got a date, haven't you?

AMBER	What do you think I am?
FRAN	No, comment!
AMBER	I'll text about the accommodation.

(AMBER *exits, the ball passing stalls to a stop. There is a lull.*)

JESS	Will we have fifteen?
MAGGIE	Will they; the last time we played them they only had ten.
JESS	And we only had nine.
MAGGIE	And we still beat them!

(*The banter is barbed but friendly.*)

JESS	Teachers; they've got an answer for everything.
MAGGIE	Like Doctors!

(JESS *collects herself, zips up her tracksuit, puts on her headphones.*)

JESS	They say this is the fastest growing women's sport in the country.
MAGGIE	That's what they say.
JESS	But that's not the case around here is it?
MAGGIE	From little acorns . . .

(JESS *is about to depart.*)

JESS	See you Saturday.

(JESS *exits. There is an awkward silence between* FRAN *and* MAGGIE.)

FRAN   What was all that about?

MAGGIE   That was about the fact that we can't recruit.

(*A beat.*)

FRAN   Well I suppose she could play anywhere.

MAGGIE   I wish she would sometimes.

(*There is acknowledgement of tension.*)

FRAN   She played at Saracens didn't she?

MAGGIE   Oh, she's hard work Fran.

FRAN   She told me that some of the girls from the hospital play at West Park.

MAGGIE   I bet they haven't got a home-made scrum machine though?

FRAN   Do they need one?

MAGGIE   They can have this one; because it won't last the season.

(*A beat.*)

FRAN   I wasn't having a dig by the . . . I know you've tried everything to get a team together.

MAGGIE   . . . I know that.

(*A beat.*)

FRAN   Well we'd better get this thing back to the facility provided then?

| MAGGIE | Absolutely! |
| | |

(FRAN *and* MAGGIE *position themselves around the scrum machine.*)

FRAN	I don't suppose there's a mini bus on the radar for this Saturday?
MAGGIE	Why, do you need a lift?
FRAN	No, I'll try and talk Colin into taking me; he can spend the morning in Blackpool.
MAGGIE	Why doesn't he come and watch?
FRAN	Have you any idea what I'll have to do just to get a lift to Blackpool?

(MAGGIE *raises her eyebrows.*)

Anyway when did Frank last come and watch?

| MAGGIE | He's chasing work. |

(MAGGIE *hobbles around but she is slightly lame.*)

FRAN	Who isn't?
MAGGIE	This bloody knee! Come on then, let's see if we can get this off.

(FRAN *goes and stands onto of the pallet.*)

FRAN	Come on, push me. Let's see what you're made of . . .
MAGGIE	You think I'm past it, don't you?
FRAN	Prove you're not!

MAGGIE	Oh here we go!
	(MAGGIE *laughs and grabs the scrum machine.*)
FRAN	Wow easy . . .
	(MAGGIE *suddenly stops.*)
MAGGIE	Right, there we go, now get your frigging self off it and give us a hand.
FRAN	There you go again, you see?
MAGGIE	What?
FRAN	Cutting corners!
	(FRAN *and* MAGGIE *pull the scrum machine off stage together. Music. Blackout.*)

Scene Four

Night. A camp site.

AMBER *enters wearing a tracksuit, and a windjammer jacket. She has with her a pop-up tent and a pack of beers and a holdall in which she secrets other beers and her overnight requirements. She is joined by* KIM *and* JESS *who are dressed in their tracksuits and who also have bags and a tent.* AMBER *has a torch and a camping light. Owls can be heard, it is very dark.*

AMBER	This is alright isn't it?
JESS	Where are we?
AMBER	I thought it'd be quiet!
KIM	We're in the middle of nowhere.

AMBER   No we're not; there's others camping over that
               fence.

               (AMBER *stands centrally and nods towards off.*)

JESS   Won't it take an age to get the tents up?

AMBER   These go up in seconds.

               (*The girls find a spot and settle with blankets.*)

JESS   What time is it?

AMBER   Ten to three.

JESS   We're actually kicking off at ten!

AMBER   You wanted to stay in the Chinese!

JESS   Only because it was warm, it's freezing out here!

AMBER   Well you and Kim can crush up.

KIM   That'd be good!

               (*There is some tension between* KIM *and* JESS.)

AMBER   Don't knock it till you've tried it!

JESS   How do you know we haven't?

KIM   Who's sharing with you then?

AMBER   Nobody, it's my tent.

               (DONNA *appears in the dark. She is has a bag
               with her, has had a few beers and has a can with
               her.*)

DONNA   Hiya.

AMBER	Eh?
DONNA	It's Donna.
AMBER	(*under her breath*) Oh hell!
DONNA	Can I join you?
AMBER	Are you sure it's not Daisy?
DONNA	She's in the car by the canal, I can't sleep in there, she's snoring like a pig; can I share?
JESS	Of course you can, you're in with Amber?
DONNA	Oh cheers Jess!
AMBER	I'm not going to sleep yet though.
DONNA	Suits me.
	(*A beat*)
AMBER	Anybody want a beer?
KIM	Why, what have you got?
	(AMBER *distributes bottles of beer which she opens with panache.*)
DONNA	Ta!
	(AMBER *does a circuit offering bottles of beer, and a bottle opener as a nurse administering to the sick.*)
KIM	And this is getting the accommodation sorted?
AMBER	It's not a real site, that's over that fence; but I went on Google Earth and saw this field next

door, why pay twelve quid a tent when we can stop here for free?

(*The girls take the bottles of beer.*)

KIM   I can't believe we're just in a field.

JESS   Martin's going to love this when I tell him.

DONNA   Is he working?

JESS   He was on call yesterday, they found a body in the Mere at Hornsea.

KIM   Well I hope these tents do go up quick Amber, I don't want to spend two hours farting about in the dark.

DONNA   That's what camping is isn't it?

(*There is gentle laughter.*)

AMBER   You don't believe me, watch.

(AMBER *demonstrates putting up a pop-up tent. She takes it from its packaging and the tent is erected immediately.*)

Ta-da!

DONNA   Wow . . .

JESS   I take it all back.

(AMBER *pulls the tent to a corner of the stage.*)

AMBER   And for my next trick . . .

JESS   Yes but how long with it take you to get down again?

AMBER   You didn't ask me that!

             (*The girls sit in a small circle and chat and
             drink.*)

KIM   They had them down in Newquay when we left
             school.

AMBER   I took it to Rugby Rocks, can't you remember?

JESS   Nobody can remember Rugby Rocks!

AMBER   I met Josh Clarke from Harlequins.

JESS   Oh yes. It's all coming back now.

AMBER   He had a run out with England under 21s.

DONNA   He had a run out with you, didn't he?

AMBER   He had something. Never seen anything like it,
             my arm was aching!

JESS   So there we go . . .

AMBER   No happy endings though.

JESS   Such a shame.

AMBER   Too pissed!

DONNA   Him or you?

             (*The girls laugh.*)

AMBER   Can you remember when we played at Worcester
             and we had to get changed in that shed?

             (*The girls are drinking easily from bottles of
             beer, a number of packets of crisps come from
             their overnight bags.*)

DONNA	Do you think the first fifteen have to camp out?
KIM	Bret would never camp.
DONNA	Where do they stop then?
KIM	Usually they have a coach or they come home, sometimes they'll do a stop over. Jack Peel sponsors them so it depends what mood he's in.
DONNA	How flush he's feeling?
KIM	Bret does some work for him, concreting.
DONNA	He's loaded isn't he, Jack Peel?
JESS	Not that we've seen any of it.
	(*The girls drink the beer easily.*)
AMBER	I thought well at least this is better than sleeping in the back of a car.
JESS	Where's the pitch?
AMBER	Just beyond the caravan site.
DONNA	So we'll be getting changed out here then?
KIM	Let's just keep drinking!
JESS	Might be worth a try!
KIM	Funds for the mini bus ran out then?
JESS	They didn't run in, according to Maggie, she was trying to get some girls who she used to teach at school the last I heard. I just hope she gets fifteen.

AMBER	Don't hold your breath!
JESS	I won't.
	(*There is easy laughter.*)
KIM	Do you think we'll win?
AMBER	Whose actually bothered, are you Donna?
DONNA	Not even thought about it.
AMBER	What about you Jess?
JESS	What?
AMBER	You always want to win don't you?
JESS	At everything, sadly, no wonder I'm stressed!
	(*There is a groan of affection.*)
DONNA	There's a girl in Scarborough who plays for the north.
KIM	The north what?
DONNA	The North of England.
KIM	Really?
AMBER	Well we need her name and number and get her down on the Scarfield.
	(*The girls drink.*)
DONNA	Hey we could buy a donkey.
KIM	For her who plays for the North?
	(*They enjoy this.*)

AMBER   Like a mascot?

DONNA   Our Daisy can get one . . . she says they were
             going to put one down, they've got it at the
             vets. We could have it branded, Scarfield Ladies
             RUFC.

JESS   We could raffle it?

DONNA   I thought it could save money on a mini bus.

KIM   Yes that'd be good; riding to a game on one!

AMBER   Jesus!

DONNA   Exactly!

JESS   It might be quicker than some of the busses
             we've hired!

             (*More laughter and drinking.*)

AMBER   Well I don't want to be too late getting back
             tomorrow to be honest, I've got a party to go to.

JESS   Another?

AMBER   A partner in the office is getting married. It's her
             third time, she's going round town. She's only
             thirty eight and she's been through three men, all
             of them loaded.

JESS   That's what we need, one of her ex-husbands!

AMBER   She bleeds them dry and leaves them for dead!

             (DONNA *looks in her luggage to see what snacks
             she has.*)

DONNA   Anybody want a pickled onion?

AMBER	Oh, don't have one of them if you're sharing with me Donna!
DONNA	Don't you like 'em?
AMBER	Ough!
DONNA	I've already had a load in the car.
AMBER	Bloody hell!
DONNA	What's up?
AMBER	Oh well done, head out of the tent!
DONNA	Are you joking?
AMBER	No I'm not bloody joking!

(The girls enjoy this.)

KIM	Can you remember when your Daisy got stranded in that port-a-loo at Newquay sevens?
DONNA	That was me, that! The England girls saw me, I locked the door and then they pushed it over and tried to roll me away.

(They find this funny.)

AMBER	Good sevens that.
KIM	Better party.
AMBER	I was so sick that morning, I couldn't play.
JESS	We know that!

| AMBER | I got one game all day, and that was only because somebody from Bristol had been rushed into A & E with food poisoning. |

| KIM | Can you remember that night on the Isle of Wight? |

| JESS | That was mission impossible! |

(They enjoy the memory.)

| AMBER | Mission Impossible? That cost me a hundred and fifty quid just to get there and we went out in the first round. |

(Variously they have finished their first bottles of beer.)

| DONNA | So have you got any more or are we going to bed? |

| AMBER | No that's it; I only brought what was in the fridge. |

| JESS | Well that's it for me. |

(A beat.)

| AMBER | Part-timer! |

| JESS | Well if there are no more . . . |

(All Groan!)

(AMBER reaches into her bag and produces another collection of bottles of beer, all the girls growl with delight.)

| AMBER | Luckily I do have a very big fridge! |

| JESS | No, not for me. |

AMBER	Oh . . . Lightweight!
JESS	Me?
AMBER	Ohhh, come on . . .
JESS	No, enough is enough.
AMBER	Oohh eh, Kim.
KIM	Dead right mate.
DONNA	Lightweight!
JESS	No way!
AMBER	Lightweight!
JESS	No!
AMBER	Lightweight!
DONNA	Lightweight, lightweight, lightweight!

(*All the girls begin to join in the chant of "Lightweight".*)

| JESS | Never let it be said! |

(JESS *stands and takes on the challenge, she takes an opened bottle of beer from* AMBER *and is about to drink it down in one.*)

| DONNA | Down in one! |
| AMBER | Drink, drink, drink, drink! |

(JESS *is about to drink when she freezes, the girls notice this and react accordingly.*)

AMBER	What's up?
JESS	What's that?
AMBER	Where?

(*The girls look off into the dark.*)

JESS	There!
AMBER	Where?
JESS	It's a bull!
KIM	It's what?
JESS	It's a frigging bull!
DONNA	Shit!
AMBER	What shall we do, Donna?

(*The girls panic and grab their belongings together slowly all eyes on the place where the bull is.*)

DONNA	Just grab your stuff slowly . . .
AMBER	I'm doing that!
KIM	Shit a brick!
JESS	Nice and easy . . .
AMBER	Now what?

(*The girls have collected the belongings and beer bottles, etc.*)

DONNA	Slowly back off . . .

*(They slowly back off. AMBER has to move
towards the tent she has erected.)*

JESS   Now what?

DONNA   Now run like fuck!

*(The girls disappear in three directions all the
tents and various items are struck from the stage.
Music. Blackout.)*

Scene Five

The training pitch. Night.

JESS, DONNA *and* KIM *charge onstage pushing the scrum machine.
The second row is made up of* MAGGIE *and* FRAN, *with* KIM *playing
scrum half. The girls position the scrum machine in the middle
of the field, they are tired and giddy with laughter.* MAGGIE *is less
than happy. She walks away from the group as they variously
giggle and get their breath back, her knee is causing her some
discomfort. It appears* DONNA *has chronic flatulence.*

MAGGIE   Very good girls; very impressive; alert the media.

DONNA   Sorry Mag, I couldn't help that!

MAGGIE   I'm not bothered about you farting Donna, I'm
                  bothered about you turning up to play under
                  my name slaughtered, if you must know what's
                  really pissed me off!

AMBER   We weren't technically pissed Mag in all
                  fairness.

MAGGIE   And then you turn up late here and fart about, the
                  lot of you!

KIM   Literally!

(*The girls are giddy with laughter*)

DONNA   I couldn't help that I've got a problem.

AMBER   Pickled onions, that!

KIM   We were attacked by a bull, Maggie!

MAGGIE   You'll be attacked by another one in a minute!

               (*There is a group groan.*)

JESS   Mag?

MAGGIE   I mean why bother?

               (*Silence.*)

               Honestly . . . why?

FRAN   Time for a group hug I think.

MAGGIE   Fuck a group hug!

               (*A beat.*)

FRAN   Time for a group fuck then? (*A beat.*) I'll get my
               coat!

MAGGIE   Jesus, Fran . . .

FRAN   Mag, come on?

               (*Silence.*)

MAGGIE   No! Honestly why do we bother?

               (*A beat.*)

AMBER	We lost because we'd had no sleep; it had sod all to do with us being pissed, and we had no sleep because we couldn't afford to stop over, simple!
FRAN	Yes we would have lost even if we had been sober. (*They find this amusing.*) I didn't mean it like that!
MAGGIE	Well I think I've had about enough tonight.
FRAN	No, come on!
	(MAGGIE *walks away from the group. There is some tension.*)
MAGGIE	It's costing me forty five pounds a week in petrol to come up here and have you lot fart in each other's faces.
JESS	That not fair!
AMBER	Come on Mag . . .
DONNA	Well I'm having awful trouble with my irritable bowel to be honest.
MAGGIE	I bloody well know that pet!
	(*The girls are still giddy.*)
KIM	I just think it's so funny!
DONNA	No don't, honestly.
MAGGIE	Right, all of you; right! Give me another dogger's lap.
FRAN	Oh no . . .
KIM	Maggie, I've got to go early!

| MAGGIE | Across the field; from here to the doggers corner; come on the farting lot of you. Come on let's make it go! And then that's it; no touch and pass, come on; off you get; come on here! |

(MAGGIE *asserts herself in a very formidable manner as* KIM, FRAN, DONNA *and* AMBER *exit reluctantly leaving* JESS *and* MAGGIE *looking at each other each other across the scrum machine.*)

| JESS | Are you okay? |

| MAGGIE | Don't patronize me! |

| JESS | I wasn't patronising anybody. |

| MAGGIE | No? |

| JESS | I'll go and join them! |

(MAGGIE *watches them jog off stage.*)

| MAGGIE | Look at them. |

(JESS *looks in that direction and is about to jog after them.* DAISY *enters in her tracksuit and is keen.*)

| DAISY | Sorry I'm late Maggie. |

| MAGGIE | Aye Daisy. |

| DAISY | Jess! |

| JESS | Hiya Daisy. |

| DAISY | Yes, sorry about all this; but I had a crippled rabbit with colitis. |

(JESS *finds this amusing.*)

JESS	Sorry!
DAISY	What?
JESS	It's just so . . .
DAISY	It's the truth!
JESS	I know, but . . .
DAISY	What's funny about that?
JESS	I just think it's the best excuse I've ever heard, sorry Daisy. We're all a bit off tonight.
DAISY	Are we scrum-aging then, or?
MAGGIE	No we're finishing early tonight.
DAISY	What?
MAGGIE	They're on a "warm down" for farting about.
DAISY	What?
MAGGIE	So there's no touch and pass?
DAISY	I can't always get here for six, that's the problem.
MAGGIE	How's your neck?
DAISY	Well I wouldn't want to sleep in a car with our Donna again, her arse is foul.
JESS	So there we go!
DAISY	So is that it then, all this way, and you're wrapping it up? What a frigging fiasco this is turning into.

(DAISY *storms off unhappily.*)

MAGGIE   Bloody hell!

JESS   She's a real talent.

MAGGIE   When she gets here.

JESS   She is though.

MAGGIE   Yes, you wouldn't want to cross her.

JESS   But you just did!

MAGGIE   She's county standard but . . . if she can't get
              here!

JESS   You need to keep hold of her.

MAGGIE   For how long, you know how it works.

              (KIM *enters breathless from the run, she has to
              adjust her tracksuit.*)

KIM   Right. I'll have to go, there's only one bus after
              nine.

MAGGIE   I thought you'd come in the car?

KIM   Mine's broken and Bret wouldn't drop me off, I
              came on the bus, my mother's got Annabelle.

MAGGIE   Well I could drop you if . . .

KIM   Donna usually goes that way but I can't wait for
              her tonight, otherwise there'll be ructions!

JESS   I can drop you back.

KIM	I'll get the bus . . . text me; let me know what's happening about the fundraising; I'll put a bucket in the salon.
	(KIM *makes her way off stage as* FRAN *enters breathless. She rests against the scrum machine.*)
FRAN	Those two got talking at doggers corner, and then they are going for a beer. I see you talked your way out of that one Jessica, nice one mate!
MAGGIE	I've missed the bloody subs now, with all this.
	(FRAN *makes to exit.*)
	You getting straight off?
FRAN	Nothing to stop for is there? Anyway Colin's booked a table for us so I can guess what he's after!
	(FRAN *exits, she is unhappy with the state of things. There is a sense of tension.*)
MAGGIE	Another happy customer . . .
	(*A beat.*)
JESS	You get it some weeks.
MAGGIE	I feel like I'm getting it every week! (*A beat.*) It wouldn't be so bad if we got a bit of support from the club.
JESS	There is that.
MAGGIE	It's all "in kind". You can't do much with "in kind".
JESS	Have you spoke to Jack Peel about it?

MAGGIE   Oh aye, he talks a good game but he's only
                interested in the first fifteen; because that's where
                the sponsorship deals are. We'll have to fund
                raise just to get to fixtures.

JESS   It's not ideal, is it?

                (*A beat.*)

MAGGIE   Anyway!

JESS   Keep swimming!

MAGGIE   That's about it.

                (*A beat.*)

JESS   Shall we put this back?

                (MAGGIE *looks at the scrumming machine.*)

MAGGIE   I think I might be losing it, I mean look at it;
                Frank thinks I've gone off the rails since Jay's
                left home. You know what; I think he might be
                bloody right. We visit her a lot, but it's not the
                same is it, and that's all petrol.

JESS   Where is she?

MAGGIE   Leeds Met, doing Sports Science. They used to
                call it PE.

JESS   They're good. Does she play?

MAGGIE   She's got absolutely no interest in rugby at all,
                bless her. She thinks it's barbaric, especially
                after what happened to her Aunt Emma. She's a
                swimmer, wants to work in Africa; that doesn't
                go down to well with Frank to be honest.

                (MAGGIE *grabs the scrumming machine.*)

Right, let's sort this monstrosity out.

JESS   I thought you'd be able to manage this on your
                own.

MAGGIE   And that's another thing pet.

JESS   What's that?

MAGGIE   I'm dropping to bloody bits, Come on then . . .

                (MAGGIE *goes to* JESS *and they form a scrumage*
                format.)

                Touch! Pause! Engage!

                (*They begin to push the scrum machine off*
                stage.)

BOTH   Feet, feet, feet, feet!

                (MAGGIE *and* JESS *strike the scrum machine, as*
                music plays. Blackout.)

Scene Six

A parkland. Day.

FRAN, AMBER *and* DONNA *enter in fancy dress, they have collection*
buckets with them. DONNA *is dressed as a pirate,* AMBER *is dressed*
as a French maid and FRAN *is dressed as a nurse, all of them in a*
saucy postcard sense of provocation. They rattle their buckets as
they enter, tired having been out on the streets all morning. AMBER
and DONNA *push* FRAN, *who is laid in a hospital bed.*

FRAN   Just park me here, out of the way. Twenty past
                they said!

                (AMBER *and* DONNA *move the bed.*)

DONNA   How much have we got?

               (AMBER *looks in her bucket.*)

AMBER   Fifty three quid, I've got.

               (DONNA *looks in her bucket.*)

DONNA   I've only got seven.

               (FRAN *inspects her bucket.*)

FRAN   I've got thirty pounds eighty but I think that's
               because of the cut-backs!

AMBER   So what's that?

DONNA   Ninety pounds eighty.

AMBER   After four hours, that's not great.

FRAN   It's better than a kick up the arse!

AMBER   Just!

DONNA   We might have earned more if we'd have let
               them kick us up the arse to be honest.

FRAN   Everyone a winner, plenty of room at the back
               lady!

AMBER   I thought I would have done better than that, fifty
               three quid, what does that say? I mean I've had
               some offers but . . .

FRAN   I bet you have dressed like that!

AMBER   You know what I mean; anyway I thought you'd
               got forty five quid?

FRAN   I did but I got those pizzas.

DONNA   Nice they were! I had anchovy.

AMBER   I don't think we were supposed to eat the
                collection, you know.

DONNA   It's not even a tenner an hour each is it? Between
                us. We'd might have been better walking the
                streets.

FRAN   We have been walking the streets unless you
                hadn't noticed.

DONNA   At least the hills are cardio.

FRAN   Yes and you got your photo in the paper.

DONNA   But that wasn't for fund raising was it? I didn't
                know they were having a pirate competition!
                Came second though; not bad.

                (*A beat.*)

AMBER   You would have thought that Jess would pay
                for a mini bus wouldn't you? And isn't Kim's
                husband loaded?

FRAN   Yes but he hates her playing.

AMBER   Why?

FRAN   Because rumour has it he's been seeing the
                doctor!

AMBER   Eh?

FRAN   That's what I've heard.

AMBER   Jess?

DONNA	You re joking!
FRAN	That's why he never comes; I think they had a bit of a . . .
DONNA	But Kim's lovely; well they both are.
AMBER	Careful Donna!
FRAN	That's the thing about Scarfield, everybody knows everybody else's business.
AMBER	How come we didn't?
FRAN	Well you don't hang about the club bar when the presidents there like the saddo I am! No good that it has ever done me.
	(JESS *enters in a white coat carrying a bucket.* MAGGIE *enters with her in a decorator overalls that she has clearly borrowed from her husband.*)
JESS	How the mighty fall!
FRAN	That's a bit obvious isn't it Jess?
JESS	It was all I could think of.
AMBER	Yes and me!
JESS	A French Maid's outfit was all you could think of?
MAGGIE	Don't even go there Jess!
AMBER	(*lost*) What do you mean?
	(*The girls burst out laughing.*)
MAGGIE	So how are we doing?

FRAN	Ninety odd quid between us.
	(JESS *considers her bucket.*)
JESS	Keerching! Ninety pounds on my own!
	(*The girls respond.*)
MAGGIE	One hundred and eighty!
	(*The girls are even more impressed.*)
DONNA	You're joking?
MAGGIE	Yes, I'm joking; eighty eight quid!
DONNA	Not bad though.
	(*A beat.*)
FRAN	Where's Kim?
MAGGIE	I thought she was coming with you?
	(*A beat.*)
FRAN	No . . .
MAGGIE	Maybe she couldn't get away what with the shop and . . .
DONNA	Maybe he wouldn't let her more like?
	(MAGGIE *feels for her purse.*)
MAGGIE	So I'm going to put twenty quid in myself.
DONNA	So what's that?
FRAN	Two hundred and odd!

(*A beat.*)

AMBER	So are you taking the bed back?
JESS	Why us?
AMBER	Well we've pushed it all along the front and up here, and anyway isn't it from your place?
JESS	I'm not pushing through the street, up here people know me!
FRAN	Well what about us, I've just seen Colin's cousins on the front, and I felt like a right tit.
MAGGIE	We'll take it if you lot want to call it a day. Thanks very much girls, well done.
AMBER	I enjoyed it!
FRAN	Yes, it's what she usually wears around town anyway!

(*They prepare to depart.*)

DONNA	Hey Mag, I had my photo taken!
MAGGIE	Oh well done pet.
DONNA	It was with that pirate with one leg; next to the Harbour Bar.
MAGGIE	I should've known!
DONNA	Good though, eh? I'm going to do outside Tesco's again. I'm parked up there, I hope it's longer than two hours? I've been there all frigging day.

(DONNA *exits and shakes her bucket as she makes her way off stage.* FRAN *swings off the bed.*)

FRAN	Right; I'll go back to A & E then.
AMBER	Be careful with that back wheel it goes all over the place; we crippled two punks on the front, didn't we?
FRAN	Come on you, let's get a beer.
AMBER	See you Thursday!
	(AMBER *and* FRAN *exit leaving their buckets on the bed. There is a moment whilst* JESS *sits on the bed, and look at their takings. There is a change in atmosphere.*)
MAGGIE	Typical isn't it?
JESS	What?
MAGGIE	Well I asked the *Evening Post* to come and cover us fundraising, I phoned the radio station and what have we got, second place in a Pirate competition! What a frigging fiasco, eh? Par for the course.
JESS	Like you say; from little acorns.
	(*A beat.*)
MAGGIE	And there was nothing in the club newsletter last week.
JESS	I don't look . . .
MAGGIE	And if you go on line; we're not even listed as a team!
JESS	We did lose . . .

MAGGIE   We turned up, and didn't cost the club a penny:
              and what gets me is that Jack Peel's spouting off
              in the paper about all the developments at the
              club.

              (MAGGIE *is struck by the impotence of their*
              efforts.)

              Oh bloody hell, eh?

JESS   What?

              (MAGGIE *sits on the bed.*)

MAGGIE   I think I might knock it.

              (*A beat.*)

JESS   Yes?

              (*A beat.*)

MAGGIE   I might just slip away.

              (*A beat.*)

JESS   Are you serious?

MAGGIE   Oh aye, I'm serious . . .

              (*Silence.*)

JESS   Because I'm definitely going . . .

              (*A beat.*)

MAGGIE   Oh, right.

JESS   I've been thinking about it for a couple of
              months . . .

MAGGIE   To Leeds?

              (*A beat.*)

JESS	They asked me at Christmas.

(*A beat.*)

| MAGGIE | Well I appreciate you staying this long. |

| JESS | Like you said; it's the way it works isn't it? |

| MAGGIE | What, creaming off the talent? |

| JESS | Well people move on. |

| MAGGIE | It's all about "Centres of Excellence" these days. |

(*A beat.*)

| JESS | I was going to mention it after Loughborough. |

| MAGGIE | West Park is it? |

(*A beat.*)

| JESS | A lot of the girls at our place . . . |

| MAGGIE | Fran told me. |

(*A beat.*)

| JESS | There are no secrets then? |

| MAGGIE | Not many. |

(*A beat.*)

| JESS | They run four ladies teams. |

| MAGGIE | Four? |

| JESS | Four full fifteens! |

(*A beat.*)

| MAGGIE | Bloody hell! |

(A beat.)

JESS   It is pretty serious.

MAGGIE   That is . . .

JESS   Yes . . .

MAGGIE   Four full fifteens?

JESS   Amazing!

MAGGIE   Bloody hell!

(A beat.)

JESS   I think you've given it a good shot here you
            know.

(MAGGIE *is philosophical but hurt.*)

MAGGIE   Yes, well . . .

            (A beat.)

            It's like you say; all the best players get creamed
            off; that's the policy they've got, how are we
            supposed to function round here?

JESS   It's never going to work.

MAGGIE   Hard going!

            (A beat.)

JESS   There isn't the critical mass. Like you said, even
            the club don't know we exist. It's a social team,
            and there's nothing wrong with that . . .

            (A beat.)

            It's not, you know . . . personal . . .

MAGGIE	No, I know that . . . it's about pitching yourself against the best there is, Jesus I understand that pet. That's where I was fifteen years ago . . . It's just . . .
	(MAGGIE *begins to cry. She is disproportionately upset.*)
JESS	Hey . . .
MAGGIE	I just feel so . . .
	(JESS *is very sensitive to* MAGGIE's *feelings.*)
JESS	Maggie!
MAGGIE	I just feel so bloody isolated!
	(JESS *moves to hold* MAGGIE, *it is very tender.*)
JESS	Hey . . .
MAGGIE	I feel like I've failed . . .
JESS	Hey!
MAGGIE	I know its bloody stupid; but I thought I could do it. I was daft enough to think it could make it work. I feel like . . . Oh eh, what a bloody joke it's been eh . . . I suppose some places are never going to get it.
JESS	It's not your fault.
MAGGIE	Look at us, I'm dressed as a bloke and I'm frigging well crying in the street! I told you I was on the bloody edge.
	(*The two women comfort each other.*)

JESS	You've done all you can . . .
MAGGIE	I didn't realise how much it bloody-well meant to me!

(JESS *holds her shoulders and it is extremely touching.*)

JESS	Of course it does . . .

(*A beat.*)

MAGGIE	So what about this two hundred quid then?
JESS	Well I suppose we could go out with a bang!
MAGGIE	Like what?

(*A beat.*)

JESS	I don't know; maybe we could organise a meal or something . . .

(MAGGIE *breaks into a lighter mood.*)

MAGGIE	A last supper?
JESS	Well, it is what they do best I suppose!
MAGGIE	Getting legless?

(JESS *and* MAGGIE *separate; things are less fragile.*)

JESS	Come on, let's shift this bed before we take root.

(*They begin to move the bed.*)

MAGGIE	You never think it's not going to work do you; you think it's got to work here; it works

everywhere else and suddenly the reality hits you. Oh dear look at me I'm off again!

(MAGGIE *is crying once more.*)

JESS   Oh, get on the bed if you're going to cry.

MAGGIE   I can't help it! Because when we go it's over for them isn't it?

JESS   It is, yes . . .

MAGGIE   I feel so much affection for them. Look at me, I mean they turn up late, they fart about, they fool around, but they're good lasses.

JESS   You're soft, you know that!

(MAGGIE *composes herself.*)

MAGGIE   Unlike you! You're ice; you have to be in your job. I'm a Primary School teacher. I cry every day because of the kind of kids I teach, they haven't got a frigging chance half of them, and we spin them such a yarn about achievement.

(MAGGIE *is able to laugh at herself, as* JESS *adjusts the direction of the bed.*)

JESS   Right then, hold on . . . I usually leave this to the nurses!

(MAGGIE *in on the bed holding the buckets,* JESS *steers the bed off stage.*)

MAGGIE   Where's Fran when you need her?

JESS   Probably in the pub!

(JESS *takes the bed off stage.*)

MAGGIE   Surprise, surprise!

                (*Music. Blackout.*)

                Scene Seven

An Indian restaurant. Night.

DONNA, FRAN, KIM *and* AMBER *bring on a long collection of tables on a truck. They return and bring on stage seven seats, which are positioned around the dining table. It is the end of a very wine-fuelled night, bottles are strewn across the table. All the girls have had a drink and are in various states of disrepair. They are thoroughly enjoying their night out, each of them able to share anecdotes and gags with equal aplomb. Remnants of a significant Indian meal remain on the table. They are all laughing near to tears as the lights fade up.*

FRAN   Oh don't!

DONNA   Can you remember when we stole that dog at
               Loughborough? That was Daisy, she took a shine
               to it.

AMBER   Yes and it had a bloody heart attack!

DONNA   And she was trying to give it CPR!

               (*This is amusing.*)

KIM   Can you remember when we played the police?

FRAN   Dirty bastards.

KIM   Gay, can you remember? They wanted to get in
               the bath with us!

FRAN   I was meaning on the field!

AMBER	What about when we played Litchfield and their captain told us that they got a giant on their team, how tall was she?
DONNA	Ten feet two . . .
AMBER	Six feet three or something, and we see her coming out with her head bobbing up and down over the top of the bushes, and we all go like, eek! And their captain looks at me and says; "That's not her!"
KIM	I can remember that.
AMBER	And then this head comes over the top of the trees.
DONNA	The trees? What is she, in a Pantomime?
FRAN	She played like she was.
KIM	Oh no she didn't!
FRAN	Oh yes she did!
	(They all groan and drink further alcohol.)
AMBER	And she was awful, wasn't she Fran?
FRAN	Not in the line-out!
KIM	Can you remember when your Daisy got caught short and she had to go in the sink at Sheffield?
DONNA	That was a mistake and all, it came off the wall!
AMBER	Where is she by the way?
DONNA	Still in the loo, she doesn't like Indian food.
FRAN	What has she come for then?

AMBER	Better call a plumber!
FRAN	Where's Maggie and Jess?
KIM	Getting another bottle of this . . . What is it?
	(KIM *looks at a bottle of wine on the table.*)
DONNA	It's nice.
AMBER	Is she paying then or is Jess treating us?
DONNA	She's good isn't she?
FRAN	She's bloody brilliant!
AMBER	So what's she playing for us for?
DONNA	They play at university, don't they? Daisy did, the woman who set Hull Ladies up was a doctor. She'd been playing since she was seven, she was my Mam's GP.
FRAN	So we need to enroll on an Open University course then, that's the secret.
	(*They are enjoying this banter.*)
AMBER	Is this coming out of subs or . . . ?
DONNA	I hope so, I'm short.
KIM	She's not asked for any this week.
FRAN	Is there a game this weekend or . . .
DONNA	She didn't say.
KIM	We need a recruitment drive!

AMBER	Oh here we go!
KIM	No, you know . . .
FRAN	Well the fund-raising was a success.
AMBER	Do you think?
FRAN	I saw Donna's photo in the paper!

(MAGGIE *enters, with a few bottles of water, and* JESS *carries two more bottles of wine.*)

MAGGIE	I've taken care of the food; but we'll have to get sorted on the drinks bill.
JESS	Yes, we couldn't afford the drinks bill.
AMBER	That's nothing new, can you remember that night in Bristol?

(MAGGIE *and* JESS *sit. There is a sudden dash for the new bottles of wine and a slight change to the tone of the evening.*)

DONNA	Are we playing this weekend then Mag?
MAGGIE	Well . . .
DONNA	'Coz I was saying to our Daisy . . .
AMBER	Was this before she went to sit in the sink?
DONNA	No, you know; just how much I'm enjoying it.
MAGGIE	Well that's good then.
DONNA	No, I mean from when I first turned up. I mean I hated sport at school; never did any, swimming, once, and now I've got a lot more confidence. I mean I know we haven't won many; but my

Mam said the other day that I'm much more confident . . . When I first joined what was I like, eh?

MAGGIE   Well?

DONNA   An absolute knob-head!

FRAN   No further comments, your honour!

DONNA   I mean we never say it; but I've never felt a part of a team before.

(*There is a group sigh of affection.*)

FRAN   So what's the gathering for, have we won the lottery or . . . ?

AMBER   Has somebody died?

KIM   Daisy might have died, she's been in there for some time.

DONNA   She'll be alright; she always makes a meal of it.

AMBER   I hope she doesn't!

(*The girls find this amusing.*)

FRAN   Which is it?

MAGGIE   Well . . . I erm . . . (*A beat.*) I think you know that I've been . .

DONNA   What?

(*The tone of the party changes, the girls sense the reason for the soirée.*)

MAGGIE   Well . . . I don't want to put too much of a downer on the party.

FRAN   But you just have . . .

AMBER   She hasn't got over the farting!

DONNA   I haven't!

            (*There is a ripple of laughter.*)

MAGGIE   Well, no, it's just that . . .

AMBER   What?

            (*A beat.*)

MAGGIE   Well I think we've tried everything over these
            last couple of years, you know, we're struggling
            to get fifteen aren't we?

DONNA   People are busy Mag, especially those on shifts, I
            mean look at tonight!

KIM   Kerry's on call and Sandy and Clare are on
            holiday.

FRAN   And we've never been able to rely on the
            students, have we?

            (*A beat.*)

MAGGIE   I just don't think . . . well what can I say?

FRAN   Well spit it out; good grief we're all adults. What,
            have you killed Frank and left him in a bin?

            (*They laugh.*)

MAGGIE   No I . . .

FRAN   Because I wish I had sometimes!

(*A huge explosion of laughter.*)

AMBER   What, killed Frank? Is there something going on
          there?

          (*A beat.*)

MAGGIE   I just think to be honest; it's time for me to . . .
          well . . .

          (MAGGIE *can't help but become very emotional,
          and the tears take over.*)

ALL   Oh . . . Mag? Hey . . .

MAGGIE   Oh God, look at me getting all bloody emotional,
          I don't know what's wrong with me!

          (MAGGIE *tries to control herself.*)

          Oh hell; I didn't want it to be like this!

AMBER   Why, what's . . .

MAGGIE   I just think we should . . . well you know . . .

FRAN   What?

AMBER   Go on . . .

          (JESS *cuts in very quickly but slowly.*)

JESS   I think what she's trying to say is that she thinks
          we are ready for another challenge. (*A beat.*)
          Aren't you?

          (MAGGIE *can't speak.*)

          You know, step it up!

(MAGGIE *is confused but even more emotional because* JESS *has done an about-face.*)

FRAN   Well that's a frigging relief; because I thought you were going to knock it. And I'd have had to find another excuse for getting away from Colin!

(*There's general good feeling.*)

DONNA   So what's the plan then, to step it up?

MAGGIE   Yes what is the plan?

JESS   Well . . .the plan is we enter a sevens.

FRAN   You see that's genius, we can't get fifteen so let's enter a sevens, why didn't I think of that? Well done Mag!

MAGGIE   Yes well . . .

JESS   It'll give us a focus and we can specialise.

KIM   Where are they though, because Bret's booked a week in Cyprus?

FRAN   Can't he go on his own?

JESS   There's one month – Bridlington, Sheffield, Ponte, Harrogate. We pick one; it's about two hundred quid to enter and the purse can be up to two grand.

KIM   Hello!

FRAN   I like it already!

JESS   So; what say; I find the entry fee and we go for it?

DONNA   Yes, sounds . . .

AMBER   Yes, hang on though; what's the alternative
               though?

               (*A beat.*)

MAGGIE   Well I think the alternative actually, is that we
               call it a day.

               (*A beat.*)

AMBER   Oh right? So it's Hobson's choice?

               (*A beat.*)

MAGGIE   Well . . .

               (*A beat.*)

AMBER   Why?

MAGGIE   Well we need to drop a pebble, don't we?

AMBER   Why, we play, we meet, we'll be putting pressure
               on ourselves.

               (AMBER *is serious for the first time and we see
               her sharp.*)

               No seriously, that's why I joined because there
               is no pressure! As a kid I was Northern Floor
               Gymnastic Champion five years running and it
               made me sick, the pressure.

MAGGIE   I understand that but –

AMBER   That's why I've stayed; and now you're saying if
               we don't step up . . .

MAGGIE   I'm just saying that if we can focus; get on the
               radar . . .

(*There is a feeling that things are
uncomfortable.*)

AMBER   What radar?

MAGGIE   Get coverage, people take us seriously.

AMBER   I don't want to be taken seriously, I get that at
             work!

MAGGIE   But you want to be recognised don't you?

AMBER   You mean marketed?

MAGGIE   Nobody knows we're here, even Jack Peel . . .

AMBER   Jack Peel's an arse!

FRAN   He's got a big arse!

JESS   I know what you're saying, but why shouldn't
             you give it a go?

AMBER   So what happens then?

JESS   I go on line, pick a seven's tournament, in a
             couple of months, let's say. We send a deposit;
             go in a pool, turn up and we play.

AMBER   Yes but who do we play?

MAGGIE   We don't know till we get there.

AMBER   Unnecessary pressure, like I said!

             (*A beat.*)

MAGGIE   I completely appreciate that if you want to say
             no, fine and we call it a day. That is honestly fine,

and I've always been honest with you. It's up to
you guys.

(*Silence.*)

JESS   Well I'm good for it!

(*A beat.*)

FRAN   Oh go on, I'm up for it, bollocks to it!

(*A beat.*)

KIM   I dunno . . .

FRAN   She'll play, you know she will. It's sevens, we
need her.

KIM   I know but –

FRAN   Oh shut up and get a drink!

(*A beat.*)

DONNA   Our Daisy will be; you know that.

(*A beat.*)

MAGGIE   What about you though, Donna?

(*A beat.*)

DONNA   Well I'll play against anybody, I don't give a
toss, any chance to knock seven bells of shit out
of somebody and I'm there!

AMBER   Yes but sevens though, it's all running!

DONNA   So what?

(*A beat.*)

MAGGIE   Well we maybe need to consider about it. (*A
beat.*) What do you think Amber?

(*Silence.* AMBER *grabs a glass and asks for it to
be filled up.*)

AMBER	I think I need another drink!
	(FRAN *fills* AMBER'S *glass.*)
FRAN	Here.
	(*Silence.* AMBER *drinks a full glass of wine in one.*)
AMBER	It's not really a choice is it?
MAGGIE	It is, it's your choice!
	(*A beat.*)
AMBER	I think it's ridiculous to be honest.
	(*A beat.*)
FRAN	And when has that stopped you doing anything?
	(*A beat.* AMBER *has another drink.*)
AMBER	You know that I hate all the frigging lot of you, you know that, don't you?
MAGGIE	Is that a yes then?
AMBER	It's as near as you're going to get!
	(FRAN *stands with a bottle and a glass of wine.*)
FRAN	Well I'll drink to that. Ladies . . . the sevens!
	(*They all raise their glasses.*)
ALL	The sevens!
	(*The girls respond with a massive cheer as they toast each other. Music plays. Blackout.*)

ACT TWO

Scene One

*Two months later. The stage has become a rugby changing room.
It is especially grim, having been in need of repair for many years.
There is no running water, and the changing room has just been
vacated by Scarfield under-fifteens rugby team who have left mud
and bandages and blood all over the floor. There are three benches
and some low lockers, there are also a number of tyres, the odd
broken chair and some perfunctory St John Ambulance first aid
equipment which is decades out of date. The set should have the
feeling of a First World War trench.*

Lights rise as MAGGIE, JESS, AMBER, KIM *and* DONNA *enter. Each
one of them has a sports bag, and a bottle of water.* MAGGIE *has
a large bag which contains the shirts and various other rugby
extras, deep heat sprays, tape, mouth guards and shoulder pads.*
DONNA *has a farming brolly. The girls are mostly dressed in
tracksuits, which represent individual tastes,* DONNA *wears Hunter
wellingtons and farm wear. In their own bags they will have boots,
a towels, shorts and shorts, each of them will wear under shorts,
which are like cycling shorts – which are underdressed – some of
them will play in gloves,* DAISY *and* DONNA *will wear scrum caps,
others may also wear scrum caps, and those who don't will wear
their hair in a bun or pony tail. As they enter they cannot help but
be disappointed with the state of the changing room.*

Silence.

MAGGIE	What?
AMBER	Nothing!
MAGGIE	Apparently we're in here because the other ones are full.
JESS	Full of what?
AMBER	Hard core then!

KIM	Can you smell that?
JESS	What's been going on?
MAGGIE	They've had an under-fifteens sevens tournament on this morning.
JESS	Nice they left it so clean!

(FRAN *enters with a small brolly. She has her sports bag and in her other hand she has two Marks and Spencer's shopping bags. She has clearly been shopping and is not in a tracksuit, she look out of place in high heels and a summer mac.*)

FRAN	Oh right. Nice! (*A beat.*) I've had to come on the train; had my shopping to do. I've been in Ponte since half ten. Me and Colin have had a difference of opinion, I think he's an arsehole and he begs to differ.
MAGGIE	And the truth is?
FRAN	It's official, he's an arsehole.
JESS	He'd feel at home in here!

(AMBER *inspects her bag and takes out a collection of baby wipes.*)

AMBER	I'll check the loo.
KIM	You mean this isn't the loo?
JESS	Don't use it!
AMBER	I've got a baby wipe . . .

(AMBER *exits, the girls look around. No one wants to start getting changed.*)

FRAN   Where's Daisy?

DONNA   Not here yet.

MAGGIE   She is coming?

DONNA   She texted me last night, said she was up for it.

                (MAGGIE *puts the large club bag centre.*)

MAGGIE   Better get changed girls!

JESS   Be careful where you put your stuff guys.

KIM   We can't get changed in here!

MAGGIE   It's here or outside . . .

                (*They find a spot and each of them proceeds to get changed slowly.*)

FRAN   And have you seen the weather?

JESS   Not perfect for sevens.

MAGGIE   That'll give us a chance then.

JESS   To get pneumonia!

                (AMBER *enters. She is not impressed by the loo.*)

AMBER   No toilet seat.

KIM   Nice!

AMBER   Better than Preston; there was no toilet!

MAGGIE   Get changed Amber pet, we're on at twenty past.

(AMBER *begins to get changed taking off her tracksuit.*)

AMBER   There's a present on the floor in there, so be careful where you stand if you go!

FRAN   That's what they think of us!

(*The girls are slowly getting changed.*)

DONNA   Actually I think I need to use . . .

AMBER   Take your Hunters!

DONNA   Don't worry about that, I'm used to it.

(DONNA *exits.*)

FRAN   And I hope she's not going to bottle it, like she did at Preston.

(MAGGIE *begins to distribute old but uniform rugby shirts, which are men's junior shirts, they are damp.* JESS *is No. 10.* KIM. *is No. 9,* DONNA *and* DAISY *are numbers 1 and 3.* FRAN *is No. 2,* AMBER*'s shirt is No. 11 and* MAGGIE *wears No. 12.*)

KIM   What pool are we in?

MAGGIE   Pool D.

FRAN   Who's in with us then?

MAGGIE   York, Halifax and the Army.

KIM   The frigging Army?

JESS   Only seven of them Kim, it's not the entire army!

MAGGIE   Here you are guys!

(*She offers a shirt to* JESS.)

JESS   These are still damp!

MAGGIE   They shouldn't be.

JESS   Well they are.

(MAGGIE *feels the shirt.*)

MAGGIE   They're not that damp are they?

(MAGGIE *gives a shirt to* KIM.)

KIM   That's damp.

MAGGIE   I think they're just cold.

KIM   No, this is damp!

(MAGGIE *gives a shirt to* AMBER.)

AMBER   Let's have a feel . . .

MAGGIE   Are they damp?

(AMBER *feels the shirt.*)

AMBER   Have you lost the feelings in your hand Mag?
                These are damp!

(DAISY *enters, she is fired up for the game. She
has a sports bag and wears a tracksuit.*)

DAISY   Come on then, where are they?

(*There is a huge cheer from the team.* DAISY
drops her bag in a space and looks around.)

DAISY   Perfect conditions!

JESS	Not in here.
AMBER	Careful in the loo, there's a turd on the floor.
DAISY	Best place for one!
AMBER	You should see the size of it!
FRAN	They're on a healthy diet then the under-fifteens!

(MAGGIE *considers the club bag.*)

MAGGIE	There's grease in the bag if . . .
JESS	And the shirts are damp.
MAGGIE	They're not damp!

(MAGGIE *gives* DAISY *shirt No. 3, which she feels against her face.*)

DAISY	This is damp!
MAGGIE	They're not that bad.
AMBER	Yes, they're not actually dripping wet.
FRAN	They will be!

(DAISY *begins to get changed. Variously the girls get shoulder pads from the club bag.*)

JESS	Who are we on with first?
MAGGIE	York Railway Institute.
JESS	Have they got seven?
KIM	Have they actually got here in this weather?

(They continue to get changed, the banter is light. FRAN *feels her shirt.)*

FRAN   These shirts are definitely damp.

JESS   Damp? Mine's soggy at the sleeves!

                (The girls go to the club bag for shoulder pads and grease for their knees and eyes, each in their own time.)

MAGGIE   Keep a strong line.

JESS   Yes! Yes!

MAGGIE   Don't get drawn.

FRAN   Is there a crowd?

MAGGIE   No idea, but we're still playing if nobody's out there!

                *(*AMBER *pulls on her damp shirt and looks in the club bag.)*

AMBER   Is there any tape did you say?

MAGGIE   In the bag.

                *(*AMBER *dips into the bag and draws out some tape for her socks, tapes up her socks and starts to put on her boots.)*

FRAN   Do the showers work or is that a daft question?

MAGGIE   Yes.

JESS   What, it's a daft question?

FRAN   That's one thing then.

MAGGIE	There's no hot water though.
ALL	Ohhh . . .
JESS	Don't tell me! The under-fifteen boys ran it all off.
MAGGIE	I don't know who . . .
JESS	Of course they did!
MAGGIE	Anyone want these?
	(MAGGIE *holds up a couple of shoulder pads. The girls have undershirts which are thermal.* FRAN *takes a pair.*)
AMBER	I'm keeping my gloves on.
FRAN	I'm keeping my raincoat on!
	(*The girls tie up their socks, pull on their boots, the sound of the boots on concrete gives a sense of the brutality to come.*)
AMBER	Is there a ball?
	(MAGGIE *scoops a rugby ball from the club bag and flips it to* AMBER.)
AMBER	We've got a ball then?
JESS	Another first!
MAGGIE	Unfair!
DAISY	Where's Donna?
AMBER	Went to the loo.
JESS	And she never came back!

AMBER	Take a baby wipe.
DAISY	It doesn't bother me, I had both hands up a cows fanny yesterday.
KIM	You should come down to the salon and have your nails done.
DAISY	It's only natural!
KIM	Who for?
FRAN	Not the cow!

(*The girls laugh easily as they get changed.*)

DAISY	All in a day's work. Are they through here?

(DAISY *exits to the loo. She is mostly changed with No. 3 shirt on her back, she pulls on a scrum cap.*)

MAGGIE	Well she's up for it!
KIM	Thank fuck!
MAGGIE	If Donna was half as good we'd be laughing.

(AMBER *drifts around the changing room with the ball.*)

AMBER	There's a leak in the roof over here, look, dripping.
MAGGIE	Keep the kicking down. Its sevens so use the ball, keep a line, man on man.

(JESS *pulls up her socks.*)

JESS	Is there any Deep Heat?

MAGGIE	In the bag!

(JESS *dips into the bag, takes out deep heat spray and tape. As she sprays the spray there is a round of coughing.*)

KIM	Do you have to?
AMBER	Does that even work?
JESS	The smell puts them off.
AMBER	Oh, my eyes!
JESS	Sorry girls!

(FRAN *dips into her shopping and pulls out a small ring-pull can of Gin and Tonic.*)

FRAN	Anyone want a tot of this?
MAGGIE	What is it?
FRAN	A G and T from Marks, I thought I'd treat myself.
MAGGIE	You can't do that!

(FRAN *drinks from the can.*)

FRAN	Give up; I'm only having a taste. Anybody?
KIM	I will.

(KIM *drinks from the can.*)

FRAN	Amber?

(FRAN *takes the can to* AMBER *who drinks.*)

AMBER	Just a little one!
FRAN	Jess?
JESS	Not today.
FRAN	Mag?

(MAGGIE *has a quick swill as* FRAN *stands by.*)

MAGGIE	Oh just a tot!

(JESS *gestures for a drink,* FRAN *takes it over.*)

JESS	Oh come here then.

(JESS *wipes the top of the can.*)

MAGGIE	We haven't got the plague pet!
JESS	Yet!

(DONNA *enters.* MAGGIE *offers her a shirt, which she pull on as she speaks.*)

DONNA	Hey they've got a barbie going out there.
AMBER	In the bog?
DONNA	Got talking to that Jennie woman who's organised it.
FRAN	Do you want a quick taste Donna?
DONNA	Just a swig.

(DONNA *takes a drink.*)

These shirts are really damp you know.

AMBER	They're not, are they?

(FRAN *takes the can from* DONNA *and finishes it off.*)

MAGGIE   I had them on the radiator all night but Frank turned the heating off; he keeps going on about the gas bill.

DONNA   When are we going to get our own shirts anyway?

KIM   Are these the under-fifteens?

              (*The girls are pulling up their laces.*)

JESS   Yes, they've just been playing in them.

MAGGIE   How are we going girls?

DONNA   We're on pitch number two, she wants us out there. She wants to try and beat the weather she says.

FRAN   Why, has the weather got a team in?

              (*The girls are still for a moment, they hold their gum shields, etc.*)

KIM   Oh shit! I've just gone all nervous!

MAGGIE   Come on!

FRAN   Where's Daisy we need here?

DONNA   She's probably out there already!

FRAN   Here we go!

              (FRAN *squashes the can.*)

MAGGIE   We ready?

(*The girls form a circle and put their arms over each other's shoulders.*)

AMBER   Here we go!

JESS   We're laying our bodies on the line for each other okay?

ALL   Okay!

MAGGIE   Enjoy every minute of it . . . yes?

ALL   Yes!

MAGGIE   Come on girls!

(MAGGIE *encourages the girls with a few motivational hugs. Each of the players hugs one in turn.* DONNA *has to pop to the loo, as she does she puts on her scrum cap.*)

DONNA   Just make a quick call . . .

AMBER   Again?

FRAN   Has she got a problem?

(DONNA *exits and straight away* DAISY *enters wearing a scrum cap.*)

DAISY   Still raining.

MAGGIE   Come on then, come on. Amber, Kim, come on Fran you old sod, come on Daisy!

DAISY   I'm coming!

MAGGIE   Come on girls, lets get out there.

DAISY   Come on.

(FRAN, AMBER KIM *and* DAISY *walk from the changing room but they are not fired, they lack any drive and seem extremely subdued.* JESS *is very fired, and is strikingly aggressive;* MAGGIE *and* JESS *are shouting at each other in a masculine fashion.*)

JESS   Alright?

MAGGIE   Yes.

              (*A beat.*)

JESS   Come on then!

MAGGIE   Come on!

JESS   Come on!

MAGGIE   Come on!

JESS   Come on, let's take them apart!

              (*The girls are ready; the gum shields go in.*)

MAGGIE   Good luck!

JESS   We're going to need it. York Railway Institute are like shit off a shovel!

MAGGIE   Good to know!

              (JESS *and* MAGGIE *exit the changing room and are charged as they do so. Music plays. Blackout.*)

Scene Two

The changing room. Twenty minutes later.

*Lights fade up. The girls enter and they are covered in mud. They
look dishevelled and are wetter than when they left. They are also
elated by their victory. They hug each other and grab a number of
drinks from their sports bags.*

DAISY	Wow!
JESS	Well played girls, keep it on!
KIM	Come on!
AMBER	Well done that girl!
FRAN	I told you that G and T would work, anybody want another?

(FRAN *helps herself to her shopping and produces
another can of Gin and Tonic.* MAGGIE *enters
the changing room and she is limping slightly. A
whistle is heard off stage from another game.*)

MAGGIE	Come on girls!
JESS	Six nil!
MAGGIE	Come on!
JESS	One down!
MAGGIE	Oh let me get one of these . . . Tramadol. Anybody else want one?

(MAGGIE *helps herself to a tablet from her sports
bag.*)

JESS	What you got there?

(DAISY *pulls a flask from her sports bag.*)

DAISY	I've got Bovril here if anyone . . .

KIM	Keep the G and T's coming!
FRAN	I am doing.
	(FRAN *opens another can of G & T.*)
JESS	Maggie?
MAGGIE	I'm okay.
JESS	You can't play on Tramadol!
MAGGIE	I have before!
	(MAGGIE *slips a tablet into her mouth.*)
FRAN	Have a taste of this, you'll be flying.
DAISY	Bovril anybody?
	(DAISY *offers her flask but drinks herself.* FRAN *opens and drinks from another can of Gin and Tonic.*)
AMBER	I thought that was your week's shopping for Colin, Francis?
FRAN	Fuck Colin.
KIM	No thanks!
FRAN	I have to!
JESS	You don't have to.
FRAN	You'd be surprised, what I have to do!
	(AMBER *takes a drink from* FRAN.)
AMBER	I like Marks, they've got some good stuff, but I think their Per Una's a bit safe.

KIM	Where's Donna?
DAISY	Got talking to a girl she knows from York.
AMBER	Oh. Oh!
KIM	Look out.
AMBER	Who's out?

(JESS *looks over at* FRAN *and her shopping.*)

JESS	What else have you got in there?

(FRAN *looks in her shopping bag.*)

FRAN	Toilet rolls, baps, chicken, pesto, some of that peppered pastrami . . .
AMBER	Oh, that's nice!
MAGGIE	Yes I like that!
KIM	Nice on a bagel.
JESS	No more Gin and Tonics?
FRAN	I've got tons of them!
DAISY	Who have we got next?
MAGGIE	Halifax.
JESS	Have you seen them?
AMBER	They look like lesbians.
FRAN	Donna should be laughing!
JESS	Keep warm, come on, hug up!

(*The girls crush together to keep warm except* FRAN.)

AMBER   There's nobody watching!

MAGGIE   As usual.

JESS   It is absolutely freezing in here!

FRAN   Hang on, what have I got here? (FRAN *brings a new bottle of brandy from her bag.*) Yes?

MAGGIE   No.

FRAN   It'll keep us warm!

MAGGIE   No!

FRAN   It'll help the Tramadol!

KIM   I don't fancy playing all day in this weather.

FRAN   That's why we're here!

AMBER   I'm here for the prize money.

MAGGIE   Come on, stay focused!

              (FRAN *puts the brandy back.*)

FRAN   No, to the brandy then?

              (DAISY *has to use the loo and exits.*)

DAISY   Must be the rain, I'll have to go again.

              (*A beat.*)

JESS   She's the difference.

MAGGIE   She's a machine!

AMBER   That's what comes from sticking your arms up a
                cows bum!

FRAN   I think she wears gloves.

AMBER   I'm wearing gloves but I don't fancy doing that!

KIM   My legs are going blue.

AMBER   I'm buzzing.

FRAN   It's the gin and tonic!

                (DONNA *enters with a shirt change.*)

DONNA   Throwing it down!

FRAN   Your kid's doing well!

                (DONNA *stands and addresses the huddle.*)

DONNA   They want us back out, Jennie's just told
                me. Richmond haven't got seven so they're
                disqualified; they can't even borrow one because
                Halifax are short; so we're straight back on.

MAGGIE   Straight back on?

DONNA   I've been looking at the draw and all; three teams
                haven't got here, so if we win the next two we go
                through to play the invitation team the way the
                draw works.

FRAN   Come on!

KIM   Legend!

MAGGIE   Oh yes!

                (*A beat.*)

AMBER	And who are the invitation team then?
	(*A beat.*)
DONNA	They're calling themselves The Black Ferns.
KIM	The Black what?
DONNA	The Blacks Ferns she says, they've got four ex-New Zealand ladies, a Tongan and two samosas!
JESS	Samoans!
DONNA	They're on a development tour, Jennie said.
	(*A beat.*)
FRAN	Eh?
DONNA	That's what she says.
FRAN	The fucking All Blacks?
AMBER	Did you know this Jess?
JESS	How could I know that? I knew there was an invitation seven but I didn't know who?
KIM	Two samosas?
DONNA	We've got to get out there guys . . . we can't piss about, otherwise they all get tetchy she said.
AMBER	Four ex-all blacks and a fucking samosa!
JESS	Come on let's eat them!
	(*There is a team groan.*)
MAGGIE	Come on, come on let's take one game at a time.

(The girls stand, they are getting cold. MAGGIE *stands and starts to galvanise her team.)*

Come on come on girls, into a huddle.

(The team go into a huddle.)

DONNA   Come on!

FRAN   Here we go!

JESS   Come on girls, this is it . . . come on ladies! Let's take them apart!

(They get themselves into a state of high energy and suddenly the bare gelling as a team. As they leave the changing room, FRAN *has a quick swig of gin and tonic and then departs.* KIM *and* JESS *exit, followed by* DONNA.*)*

DONNA   The shirts are damp now aren't they Mag?

MAGGIE   They will be by the end of today!

AMBER   I just hope we don't fucking win.

MAGGIE   Come on!

AMBER   Let's take a dive shall we?

MAGGIE   Come on, focus!

AMBER   I bet she knew about this; didn't she?

*(*MAGGIE *and* AMBER *take a step towards the exit. They are apprehensive. Music. Blackout.)*

Scene Three

The changing room. Twenty minutes later.

The girls return, they are breathing heavily as the weather and the effort is beginning to take its toll. All of them take a seat, they are breathless and battered. AMBER *is the last to arrive in the changing room, she has been slightly concussed and has two tampons stuck up her nose, which she holds delicately. She is more covered in mud and wetter than previously.*

AMBER	What a fucking fiasco this is . . .
JESS	Are you okay?
AMBER	Do I look okay with two tampons stuck up my nose?
MAGGIE	You should tuck your head in when you tackle.
	(*The girls sit,* AMBER *wanders around. She is very unhappy.*)
AMBER	I did.
JESS	You didn't, you fell to your knees and shouted; "watch my face!"
KIM	And then you got it!
	(AMBER *is fired by the indignation.*)
AMBER	Look at me; I look like a freak show!
JESS	They're just to stem the bleeding.
AMBER	Bleeding, she nearly took my head off!
	(*The girls drink from water in their bags and wipe themselves down without muddying the towels.*)
MAGGIE	It was a bit high.

AMBER	A bit high, she was looking for me!
DONNA	Maybe she fancied you?
AMBER	Well I didn't fancy her.

(MAGGIE *takes a few more tablets secretly,* JESS *notices this.*)

JESS	What're you doing?
MAGGIE	They don't touch me!
AMBER	What a pissing disaster!

(AMBER *feels her nose tentatively.*)

FRAN	We won. What're you on about?
AMBER	I'm on about me looking like a walrus, and I didn't want to win!

(KIM *considers the colour of her legs.*)

KIM	My legs are blue, look at that; twenty five quid for a spray tan and it's just gone.
AMBER	Well at least you haven't got a tampon up your nose.
KIM	Yet!

(*The girls adjust their kit.*)

JESS	We can't play down the left hand side, keep it up the middle.

(DONNA *looks in her bag and produces some food.*)

DONNA	Anybody want a bite? I've got a pork pie . . . Rhubarb and pork . . . they're awarding-winning. I got them from the farm shop before my Mum got up . . . anybody?
FRAN	I'll have a taste.

(DONNA *offers* FRAN *a bit of a pork pie, which she cuts with a camping knife.* DONNA *looks in her bag.*)

DONNA	And there's a bit of black pudding if . . .
KIM	I'm veggie, so . . .
MAGGIE	Not for me.
JESS	No thanks.
AMBER	I'll have a little slice . . .
FRAN	Has the bleeding stopped?
AMBER	The humiliation hasn't!

(DONNA *is in her bag, offers a piece of black pudding to* AMBER, *and goes back to her bag.*)

Ta! Mmmm!

DONNA	Oh sorry that pie's not rhubarb Fran, it's beetroot, this is the rhubarb, this is the award-winner. I don't know what the hell that one is.

(FRAN *chews of a piece of pie.*)

FRAN	So I'll probably get food poisoning, perfect!

(*A phone rings with a strange ringing tone.*)

MAGGIE	Who has left their phone on?

KIM   Sorry guys.

                     (KIM *is on the phone to her husband whilst the
                     other girls can't help but listen but continue to
                     drink and eat and adjust their kit.*)

                     Hey! (*A beat.*) No, you know where I am. Well I
                     can't talk here. Jesus!

MAGGIE   Keep warm guys.

KIM   (*on the phone*) Why? What?

FRAN   Nice pie.

KIM   (*on the phone*) Well we're through to the next
                     round because some teams haven't . . .

DONNA   That black pudding alright?

KIM   (*on the phone*) Bret?

AMBER   So we're throwing the next game right?

JESS   What?

AMBER   I don't want to play the samosas, alright?

JESS   Honestly, I had no . . .

KIM   (*on the phone*) You knew I was coming here
                     though. (*A beat.*) Well? Bret? Bret? (*A beat.*) It's
                     every month I get this and it's not fair! (*A beat.*)
                     Oh well sod you then!

                     (*She puts the phone down and is very upset.
                     Silence.*)

                     He says he's going . . . again!

(*The girls are aware of the conversation.*)

Maggie	Hey Kim, pet . . .
Jess	I'm sure he's not . . .

(Kim *is suddenly angry and emotional.*)

Kim	Oh leave it you!
Jess	Hey . . .
Kim	Hey what?
Amber	Well you're better off without him anyway.
Kim	How would you know?
Amber	Well . . .
Kim	You go through men like you're going through tights.
Amber	I don't go through tights.
Kim	He's says he's seeing somebody.
Jess	Well it's not me so . . .
Kim	Well it's somebody.
Jess	Well it's not me!
Amber	For God's sake you two!
Kim	How do I know?
Jess	What?
Kim	Because I know you've been seeing him . . .

JESS   You what?

KIM   I know all about it Jess!

AMBER   Well if she has she's not the only one is she?
                He's been putting it around all the women in the
                club if you want to know!

JESS   I didn't do the running Kim!

AMBER   And he's not my type, so it's not me.

DONNA   And it's not me!

FRAN   No comment.

                (KIM *places her phone back in her bag.*)

KIM   He says he's going this time.

FRAN   I wish that fucker of mine would go and never
                come back!

KIM   My husband has just walked out . . .

AMBER   They're not worth the trouble . . .

KIM   Oh shut it; what do you know?

AMBER   I know I'm pregnant so . . .

JESS   What?

                (JESS *hears this but is compromised by her
                profession. She stands and shrugs her disbelief.*)

AMBER   Oh leave it!

JESS   How many weeks?

(DONNA *watches the action stuffing herself with a pork pie.*)

DONNA   Fuck me!

JESS   Should you even be playing?

AMBER   I shouldn't be playing with a tampon up my nose!

MAGGIE   Hey hey . . . guys.

                 (DONNA *casually chips in.*)

DONNA   Whose is it then?

AMBER   Oh give up!

JESS   Take it easy . . .

AMBER   When they're trying to take my head off?

DONNA   (*still eating the pork pie*) It was high that tackle!

KIM   (*very distressed*) What am I going to do?

MAGGIE   Aren't we frigging well-blessed?

DONNA   I'm gunna t' bog.

                 (DONNA *exits eating the pork pie. Things are extremely tense in the changing room.*)

                 Help yourself to some pork pie Kim if you want.

                 (JESS *goes to* KIM. KIM *is very upset.*)

JESS   Hey . . .

KIM   What?

JESS	We had a couple of coffees.
KIM	Oh yes?
JESS	That's all . . .
KIM	Really?
JESS	He's got a problem Kim, if you want to know the truth.
KIM	And now I have!
JESS	I'm not shagging your husband.
KIM	Well somebody is, and it isn't me!
JESS	Well it isn't me either!
FRAN	And it's not me! I don't like him, I think he's a twat.
	(MAGGIE *is becoming angry.*)
MAGGIE	This is with you plying everybody with drink.
FRAN	It's not me who's got her pregnant is it?
	(DAISY *enters in a state. She grabs her bags and begins to depart.*)
DAISY	I have to go girls, sorry!
JESS	What?
MAGGIE	'You doing?
DAISY	I've got to go!
MAGGIE	What?

DAISY   Sorry!

               (DAISY *begins to get changed so she is
               presentable. She finds her car keys and her
               phone.*)

FRAN   What's happening?

DAISY   Adam's texted me.

AMBER   How did he do that?

DAISY   I've got a pager down my sock! No one else is
               available, there's a horse in breach near Thorpe
               Arch. The weather's making the animals play up
               and I can't body swerve it, sorry guys.

               (DAISY *has almost collected all her belongings,*
               MAGGIE *is frustrated and anxious.*)

MAGGIE   We might be playing the Black Ferns!

DAISY   They're not the real Black Ferns are they, and
               you're not through yet anyway so . . .

MAGGIE   And we won't be without you.

DAISY   Well lose the next game then.

JESS   And miss a chance to play against them?

               (DAISY *walks out with her phone and her bag in
               her hand. She notices a pork pie and grabs that
               as she leaves.*)

DAISY   You never know when you're going to get some
               lunch; sorry guys. Have fun!

               (DAISY *has gone. The team is in tatters,* MAGGIE
               stands and is furious.)

MAGGIE   What a bloody . . .

FRAN   Fantastic!

KIM   That's it then for me.

                (DONNA *immediately enters. She is bemused.*)

DONNA   She got a call out?

                (KIM *grabs her bag and prepares to leave.*)

KIM   I'm going!

                (JESS *shouts and controls the panic.*)

JESS   Hey come on keep focused or somebody will get
                hurt.

KIM   Bit late for that isn't it?

FRAN   It's like the bloody Social Service offices in here!

KIM   (*almost hysterical*) I can't stay here and pretend
                nothing's happened!

AMBER   Somebody slap her!

DONNA   (*still eating*) I'll slap her if you want.

FRAN   I can slap her if you want.

KIM   It's not me who needs slapping!

                (*These remarks are thrown away lightly.*)

MAGGIE   If anybody is going to be slapping anybody it'll
                be me.

JESS   (*quite controlling but strong*) Shit happens Kim.

AMBER	It does in here!
KIM	(*very emotional and agressive*) I could kill you!
JESS	Nothing happened, he wanted it to but it didn't. He hasn't left you for me.
KIM	(*screams*) Well it's somebody and I'm here in this mess!
	(*The sound of thunder outside.*)
FRAN	Listen to that.
AMBER	Just what we want.
DONNA	I've brought a brolly so . . .
JESS	Well we all can't get under it!
FRAN	We could put a bag on our heads.
AMBER	And that wouldn't be the first time.
	(MAGGIE *stands and holds* KIM, *and tries to calm her down.*)
MAGGIE	Come on kid! Come on pet. Kim, come on . . . eh?
	(MAGGIE *takes hold* KIM *who stands emotionless.* JESS *offers a kind of apology.*)
JESS	We had a couple of coffees that's all . . .
	(JESS *stands.* MAGGIE *gestures she lets it go.*)
MAGGIE	Jess, leave it leave it.
JESS	I resent the fact . . .

MAGGIE   Leave it eh?

                (*A beat.*)

FRAN   Group hug anybody?

                (KIM *manages a smile as* MAGGIE *hugs her.*)

KIM   Piss off!

                (*The girls have to laugh, it is so insane an idea.*)

FRAN   I'm serious, come on, group hug!

                (FRAN *stand powerfully and gestures for all the
                team to get a grip and come together.*)

                Donna, Amber, Jess, Kim, come on Mag, hobble
                over here.

                (FRAN *loses her temper since no one is taking her
                seriously. It is shocking.*)

                I said come here now, all of you!

                (FRAN *threatens all the girls to come together in
                the middle of the dressing room and bury their
                differences. The girls hug each other in a circle;
                they are exhausted and covered in rain and mud
                and emotionally shattered. However, they will
                regroup and fight on.*)

                Come on girls let's keep together, let's keep it
                together.

                (*They hug each other and squeeze each other
                tightly.*)

DONNA   Shit!

MAGGIE   Come on guys focus eh?

DONNA   Oh shit!

MAGGIE   Come on!

DONNA   I can't believe we're playing the army!

KIM   I can't believe that he's just walked out!

MAGGIE   Come on, let's go and see what they've got.

AMBER   Let's lose it shall we? Let's just let them win.

             (*The girls try to galvanise themselves into going
             out for the game against the army.*)

JESS   We go right, we go and we take the army them
             apart!

AMBER   Let's just let them win!

JESS   Come on!

             (JESS *screams before putting in her gum shield.*
             AMBER *puts in her gum shield and takes the
             tampons from up her nose and throws them
             onto the floor, they are emotional and quiet but
             focussed.* JESS, DONNA, FRAN *and* AMBER *exit,*
             MAGGIE *and* KIM *remain momentarily.*)

KIM   What am I doing here, what am I doing?

MAGGIE   Come on pet. Come on!

             (*Music. Blackout.*)

                        Scene Four

The changing room. Twenty minutes later.

The girls enter with real energy, they have beaten the army in a
very difficult match. They are now absolutely covered in mud, their
faces and their knees, their shirts in some cases, are completely
covered. KIM is exhausted, angry and elated, she cannot get her
breath and is in the throes of a panic attack.

KIM   Oh, hell. Hell, I can't get my breath!

               (KIM *is bent double, she is in panic mode.*)

MAGGIE   Well played Kimbo!

AMBER   I thought we were going to let them win?

               (JESS *comforts* KIM.)

JESS   Just breathe; concentrate on the breaths.

KIM   Oh!

               (DONNA *heads for her bag.*)

DONNA   Bring it on eh?

KIM   Oh!

               (FRAN *looks in her shopping bag.*)

FRAN   Anybody for another G and T?

               (FRAN *digs deep into her shopping,* JESS *tries to*
               comfort KIM.)

JESS   Oh leave it Fran, no more.

FRAN   Fuck off, you!

               (KIM *is getting her breath back.*)

KIM   I just kept running, I was waiting for the whistle.

JESS	At least you remembered to put the ball down.
AMBER	I've never seen anybody that quick!
MAGGIE	It helped that the dog was on the pitch!
JESS	Yes who let that dog on?
FRAN	Big, wasn't it?
AMBER	I thought it was coming for me.
KIM	I never saw a dog . . . I just kept running!
	(JESS *and* KIM *are calmer,* AMBER *plays with her nose.*)
AMBER	I think I've got some string from the tampons stuck up my nose.
MAGGIE	I took a right crack on my shoulder, feel a bit light-headed.
JESS	That's the Tramadol!
	(MAGGIE *sits, there is a moment's repose.*)
MAGGIE	Oh I've been worse than this, I played stoned at Loughborough in the eighties. I scored two tries against Cambridge in a trial. I played in the fog once and had no idea who we were playing, never saw the ball.
	(DONNA *is tired as are all the team.* KIM *sits, she is calmer.*)
DONNA	We're a team of sex maniacs and drug addicts.
MAGGIE	Not far off!
DONNA	I mean I've had to have two asprin this morning.

AMBER   Yes, I'm on antibiotics.

KIM   I am!

FRAN   We beat the army!

AMBER   I know, I can bloody can't believe it!

MAGGIE   Well done Kimbo, what a try . . .

JESS   Really good.

KIM   I just kept going . . .

MAGGIE   Oh hell . . . What a bloody day.

FRAN   What a muddy day as well Maggie!

MAGGIE   Abso-bloody-lutely!

               (DONNA *looks in her bag.*)

DONNA   Anybody got any room for a bit of sponge cake?

               (*There is a choric groan.*)

FRAN   Oh go on then.

DONNA   My Mum made it.

AMBER   Do you think they're really ex-all blacks?

MAGGIE   They look like they are!

JESS   It doesn't matter does it, it'll be good to just go
               out and see what they're like.

AMBER   No it won't, not for me.

| MAGGIE | In these conditions it doesn't matter, its poor rugby. We only beat the army because the ball's like a bar of soap! |

AMBER   And Kim's like a bullet!

MAGGIE   They won't be able to play their normal game, so
           we've got a chance.

           (DONNA *gets some cake out.*)

DONNA   My Mum makes it; kept really nice in here.

FRAN   That's the damp!

MAGGIE   Thirty minutes then we're done girls, let's keep it
           together for this last one.

           (*A beat.*)

FRAN   Then we'll all need a week in Cyprus!

           (*They are becoming more settled.*)

AMBER   Can you remember when nobody turned up at
           that tournament in Sheffield and we won the
           Stuart Burchill trophy?

JESS   Whoever he is.

AMBER   We only won that because none of the other
           teams could make it; hadn't they all got diverted
           because of the road works or something?

MAGGIE   They'd had a blow out.

JESS   And your point is?

AMBER   It was an easier way to win, that's what I'm
           saying.

KIM   Well obviously because we were the only team to
               turn up!

JESS   Yes but if you don't ever test yourself . . .

               (*A beat.*)

AMBER   Hey I tell you this much; the army are fit aren't
               they? I mean I know we won but . . . uph!

FRAN   It's a good job they are though isn't? That's what
               we want them to be; we don't want them to be
               like the lazy sods in our office, sat about dunking
               ginger nuts, and going early on a Friday.

               (*There is real calm for the first time, and humour
               is returning.*)

MAGGIE   Talk about fit. I went back to Loughborough
               three months ago. They're doing a plaque thing
               for Emma.

FRAN   That's nice.

MAGGIE   I'd forgotten what it was like.

JESS   Yes?

MAGGIE   It's like Athens; people running everywhere.

               (*A beat.*)

KIM   I think I'm going to call him back.

               (KIM *looks for her phone and stands.*)

FRAN   He's a twat Kim, leave him.

KIM   I want to tell him we're playing some of the
               Black Ferns!

FRAN   He won't leave you, you've got Annabelle; he's
              just a frigging arse.

KIM   I'll just leave a message.

              (KIM *begins to exit.*)

AMBER   It's teaming it down out there.

              (KIM *exits. The girls look at each other.*)

DONNA   Shall I go with her?

MAGGIE   Give her some space.

              (*A beat.*)

JESS   Shit happens.

              (*A beat.*)

AMBER   Yes, but was it shit?

JESS   Absolutely nothing happened.

AMBER   Oh yes.

JESS   He's a maniac! A complete . . .

FRAN   Twat!

JESS   Exactly.

FRAN   I've seen him in the clubhouse. Unbelievable.

MAGGIE   Hasn't he got a cement business?

AMBER   And I think he's been laying it all up the coast.

JESS   Honestly; hormone imbalance or something.

(*A beat.*)

FRAN	She should have never married him.
AMBER	There speaks a woman with experience.
FRAN	I wouldn't touch him with a barge pole.
AMBER	He probably wouldn't want you to.
FRAN	He can keep his big knob in his trousers.
AMBER	You've heard the same stories then?
FRAN	I'd like to grab him by it and swing him around my head!

(*The girls laugh as the image.*)

MAGGIE	Well I'd pay good money to set that Fran, pet.
DONNA	Is that what you do with Colin?
FRAN	Every night! He's dizzy with it, doesn't know where he is, then I lock him in a cupboard and curl up on the sofa.

(*The banter is easy and appreciated.*)

DONNA	Well, we're here girls.
FRAN	Just.

(*A beat.*)

DONNA	Bet you're glad you're here now, eh Amber?
AMBER	No.
JESS	She is!

(DONNA *laughs.*)

DONNA   I bet you're glad you got a team together though, eh Mag?

MAGGIE   I'll be glad when this knee stops playing up.

              (*A beat.*)

DONNA   Why did you?

MAGGIE   What?

DONNA   I was saying to Daisy . . .

FRAN   Don't you know?

DONNA   Know, what?

              (*A beat.*)

MAGGIE   I did it because of Emma.

DONNA   Who?

MAGGIE   My sister, I thought everybody knew. Why?

DONNA   Does she play?

MAGGIE   She did.

DONNA   Does she not?

              (*A beat.*)

MAGGIE   She died . . .

DONNA   Oh . . .

              (*A beat.*)

MAGGIE   Yes.

DONNA   Sorry . . .

                (*A beat.*)

MAGGIE   She had a head injury in a trials match; blood
                clot.

                (*A beat.*)

DONNA   I'm sorry.

                (*A beat.*)

MAGGIE   And she was brilliant, wasn't she Fran?

FRAN   She was, yes!

                (*A beat.*)

MAGGIE   Twenty five . . .

DONNA   I'm ever so . . .

                (*A beat.*)

MAGGIE   That's why I wanted to start a ladies team.

DONNA   I had no idea.

                (*A beat.*)

MAGGIE   Oh yes; a county player, played for the North,
                played for England.

FRAN   They couldn't get anywhere near her!

DONNA   Really?

                (*A beat.*)

MAGGIE	I asked Jack Peel if he would help support a ladies team at Scarfield and he said he would.
JESS	But he never has.
MAGGIE	Well, not yet.
JESS	So what does that say about him?
MAGGIE	That he's all wind and water!
FRAN	Like where he builds his houses!
MAGGIE	In fairness, without Scarfield we wouldn't have even got it off the ground. It's so difficult. And I'm still waiting for him to find us some money for our own shirts.
	(*A beat.*)
FRAN	It's a sore point Donna.
	(*A beat.*)
DONNA	So it should be.
MAGGIE	We need to develop new players.
DONNA	We do and all!
MAGGIE	And you know why, don't you?
	(*A beat.*)
DONNA	Well . . . no, not really.
MAGGIE	Because you never know where they're going to come from, Donna.
DONNA	That's right.

MAGGIE   And that's the same for any talent; you never
              know where it's going to come from.

              (*A beat.*)

DONNA   I'm sorry for asking Ma –

MAGGIE   I'm not, I'm not sorry you asked; because I need
              to be reminded why I'm doing it.

DONNA   Yes?

              (*A beat.*)

MAGGIE   It's the resentment Donna pet; that keeps me
              going.

DONNA   Resentment?

              (*A beat.*)

MAGGIE   Why did it have to happen to my sister?

              (KIM *enters sheepishly and puts her phone back
              into her belongings.*)

AMBER   You speak to him then?

KIM   Yes.

AMBER   Weak!

KIM   He's alright really.

JESS   Argh!

FRAN   We take it all back.

              (*A beat.*)

KIM	They want us out there. They're coming out but it's as black as hell. I think there's going to be another downpour.

(MAGGIE *stands and is rather fired.*)

MAGGIE	Dry your hands then girls.
JESS	Yes, dry your eyes as well.
MAGGIE	Yes and dry your eyes.

(*The girls can't help but find this sarcasm extremely funny and they crack into a warm and uniting laugh.*)

Come on then Ladies! Let's give it to them for Emma! Come on Donna, let's see what you can do.

(MAGGIE *hugs* DONNA.)

Watch my back . . .

DONNA	Sorry!

(MAGGIE *hugs* FRAN.)

MAGGIE	Come on you drunken old sod.
FRAN	Takes one to know one!

(MAGGIE *hugs* AMBER.)

MAGGIE	What are you like?
AMBER	You tell me.

(MAGGIE *hugs* KIM.)

MAGGIE	Come here!

(MAGGIE *hugs* JESS.)

JESS   Let's do this.

MAGGIE   Black Ferns, here we come!

FRAN   Shit!

AMBER   Awesome!

KIM   Oh hell.

DONNA   Arrgh, come on then . . . hit me, hit me.

AMBER   I'll hit you.

FRAN   Here, I'll hit you.

DONNA   Hang on, I'll hit myself!

                (DONNA *slaps herself around the face.*)

                Come on!

MAGGIE   Come on let's do this . . . come on girls let's do
                this!

                (MAGGIE *inspires her team to get out and play the
                Black Ferns. The weather is bad, thunder cracks
                as we hear their rugby boots on the cold concrete
                floor as they go out to play some of the best
                players in the world. Music. Blackout.*)

Scene Five

The changing room. Twenty minutes later.

*The girls enter, they are now completely soaked and mud covered,
completely dejected and the silence is deafening. They are all*

angry and shocked, they either sit in tears or stand in silence, they have transcended the cold but they are caught in a vacuum. There is a real atmosphere in the changing room which could be cut with a knife. MAGGIE *stands and slowly animates, she is lost for words.*

MAGGIE	What was that all about?
JESS	Leave it!
MAGGIE	There was absolutely no reason to do that!
FRAN	Just leave it Mag!
MAGGIE	Absolutely no reason!
KIM	Oh shit a brick . . . after all the frigging effort!
MAGGIE	Why would you do that?
FRAN	She's got a point . . .
	(*A beat.*)
MAGGIE	Why would he stop the game just like that?
	(*A beat.*)
AMBER	Well how about the fact that we couldn't see a hand in front of us?
MAGGIE	There were only six minutes left to play! Six minutes, he could have played on for another six minutes surely! Why did he stop the game with six minutes to go?
KIM	Well maybe because we couldn't see the ball?
DONNA	I'd never seen rain like it!
FRAN	That's an understatement, that.

KIM   Couldn't see a thing.

               (*A beat.*)

AMBER   They were strong and all weren't they, it was like
               playing men. I got a few tackles in but . . . oh my
               shoulders . . .

FRAN   Solid!

AMBER   It was like playing men.

               (*A beat.*)

JESS   I think two of them were men, to be honest . . .

MAGGIE   Seven-three to them and he stops the game?

KIM   Well we didn't lose.

DONNA   But we didn't win.

MAGGIE   He shouldn't have stopped the frigging game!

FRAN   Yes but, Mag, we were losing.

MAGGIE   That's not the point! That's not the frigging
               point! He should have let us play on.

FRAN   (*exhausted*) I'm knackered.

MAGGIE   Would he have stopped a man's game? No!
               Would he have stopped an under-eighteens, no!
               An under seventeens no, an under-twenty-ones
               no, he stopped the game because of who we are!

               (*A beat.*)

AMBER   Maybe he was worried about his toupee
               shrinking! (*A beat.*) I'm serious, it looked in a
               right state.

KIM	Well whose bothered anyway?
MAGGIE	Me, I'm bothered! If it had been a men's game we would have played to the final whistle.
FRAN	Not in that weather.
MAGGIE	I've played in worse than that!
AMBER	Where, Rangoon?
MAGGIE	He should've let us play on.
AMBER	Why?
MAGGIE	Because he would have respected us then.
	(*A beat.*)
FRAN	I thought we did well.
AMBER	I'm just glad we're alive; we should have never been on the same pitch as them.
	(JESS *takes exception to this view.*)
JESS	Bollocks to that, we're as good as them; we're as good as them, right! I'm as good as them.
AMBER	Alright, alright, calm down; I'm only saying, take a chill pill.
	(JESS *has shown too much of her emotions.*)
FRAN	Right, well; I suppose a shower's out of the question?
	(*The girls are completely out on their feet.*)
KIM	Kinnel!

MAGGIE	No water, no kit, the changing room is a toilet, no coverage in the paper and he stops the game for no reason. Why bother, why bother?
JESS	And nobody watching.
AMBER	They're all in the bar.
FRAN	Watching the footy, probably.

(*A beat.*)

AMBER	Well, I'm completely shagged!

(DONNA *looks at her gum shield and feels in her mouth as she drifts around the changing room.*)

DONNA	I'm bleeding in my mouth; must have bit my gum shield.
KIM	I couldn't see the ref, could you?
FRAN	I couldn't see a thing.
MAGGIE	He shouldn't have stopped the match. I'm going to write to somebody about it.
AMBER	Because that always makes a difference!
JESS	We need a top solicitor on the case.
AMBER	Ha-ha!

(FRAN *begins to stir.*)

FRAN	I think there's a free bar, just to bring us back to earth.

(FRAN *wraps a towel around her mud-soaked kit, and grabs her bags.*)

Feel like I've been on the sands, right, I'm up there for a beer, anybody?

JESS   You going like that?

FRAN   Well if there's no showers.

AMBER   You going back on the train?

FRAN   I'm going to get a drink first.

AMBER   So what happens to the two grand then?

JESS   That's a good call!

AMBER   Will they split it?

MAGGIE   It'll disappear into some hole somewhere.

AMBER   You should write about that as well.

            (FRAN *is lurking with her belongings.*)

FRAN   There's another gin and tonic if anybody . . . I'll see you Thursday then girls. Are we training?

MAGGIE   I'll text you.

FRAN   See you then, see you Mag . . .

            (FRAN *moves to exit.*)

MAGGIE   See you Fran . . .

FRAN   I'll wash the shirt myself. If I can get it off, I'm desperate for a beer!

MAGGIE   Cheers mate!

FRAN   See you sweetheart!

JESS   Cheers Fran!

                     (*The girls start to peel of their shirts, and toss
                     them centrally towards the club bag.*)

KIM   I'm going to get off, my Mum's come for me.
                     She's probably in the bar with Annabelle. See
                     what she's got to say . . .

                     (*A beat.*)

                     Shirts in the facility provided Mag?

MAGGIE   Just leave them, I'll get it all sorted.

                     (KIM *exits.*)

KIM   See you later; yes.

                     (AMBER *stands and collects her stuff.*)

AMBER   I'm going up to the bar for one or two.

JESS   You need to see a doctor!

AMBER   Oh shut up you, what do you know?

                     (AMBER *moves to exit.* DONNA *drifts around the
                     changing room.* JESS *and* MAGGIE *remain seated.*)

JESS   Take it easy.

                     (AMBER *is about to exit the changing rooms.*)

AMBER   I'm out tonight for a party.

                     (AMBER *exits.* MAGGIE *nurses her knee which is
                     very painful.* DONNA *begins to assemble her bags,
                     pork pies and various bun cases.*)

DONNA	You should see somebody about that knee you know Maggie.
JESS	I've told her that!
MAGGIE	But what does she know?
DONNA	Yes, she's only an expert!
JESS	Why do I bother?

(MAGGIE *smiles as this is played back to her.*)

DONNA	My Dad had a dodgy knee and he didn't have it seen to and he never played again.
MAGGIE	Cheers Donna.
DONNA	Just for facts. (*A beat.*) He's in a chair now; and me and my Mam do the farm.

(*A beat.*)

A good job he called it off really; we were dead on our feet! And they were good weren't they?

MAGGIE	Yes!
DONNA	I thought they were very good.

(*A beat.*)

MAGGIE	They were alright.

(*A beat.*)

DONNA	I thought they were good, especially that samosa.

(DONNA *is about to leave.*)

There's a muffin left if you . . . See how Daisy's
gone on. See you!

(DONNA *exits, covered in mud.* JESS *and* MAGGIE
*sit in silence, they are both exhausted, wet
and covered in mud, emotional and tired.*
JESS *removes her shirt with a struggle and
places it near the club bag, she has a thermal
underneath.*)

JESS   I'd better make a move . . . (JESS *start to collect
her belongings.*) What are you doing?

MAGGIE   Frank's coming for me on his way back.

JESS   How long will he be?

MAGGIE   No idea.

JESS   You could be here all afternoon!

MAGGIE   We're going to call at Leeds and see Jay. (*A
beat.*) Put your shirt in the bag, I'll sort it.

                (JESS *continues to get changed as best she can
                with the wet and mud.*)

                Thanks, by the way.

JESS   For what?

MAGGIE   For not letting me pack it in.

JESS   I couldn't, it means too much to you.

                (*A beat.*)

MAGGIE   Well I don't think we'll be setting the world of
Ladies Rugby on fire up at Scarfield, but . . .

                (*A beat.*)

JESS	Well West Park would love you to have you over there if . . .
MAGGIE	. . . I bet they've never heard of me!
JESS	They know all about you.
MAGGIE	How come?
JESS	Emma told them, she said you were the best player she'd ever seen.

(MAGGIE *is tearful once more.*)

MAGGIE	Sisters, eh?
JESS	It's worth a thought.
MAGGIE	It's the petrol money though pet. Frank would go mad; he'd lose what little hair he's got!

(*A beat.*)

JESS	Four ladies teams!
MAGGIE	That is a set up.

(*A beat.*)

JESS	And you need to see somebody about that knee, and stay away from the Tramadol.
MAGGIE	I live on it!

(*A beat.*)

JESS	Suppose, I might see you about.

(*It is awkward for them.*)

You never know your luck!

(Jess *concludes her changing and exits with little feeling.* Maggie *sits alone. She stands and is hobbling. She starts to collect the shirts and little bits of tape and shoulder pads and other things which have come out of the club bag including the ball. She sits and takes off her own shirt; it is very painful for her. Her phone rings.*)

Hiya darling? How long with you be? Another hour and a half? No, no problem. I thought we were going to Leeds? No, I know there's nothing you can do about it Frank. No, no they cancelled the game because of the weather . . . well how the hell could I have known that they'd do that Frank, talk sense?

(*A beat.*)

So I'll just sit tight then, will I? No you've got to finish the job pet, no I don't want you cutting corners. Give us a text when you . . . okay . . . you get on with it . . .

(Maggie *puts the phone down, she is ever so low. She holds up some of the mudded and wet shirts and recommences packing the club bag. She aches and holds her back and rubs her knee, bends once more and slowly packs the club bag. As she does* Jess *enters with two pints of beer in plastic glasses.*)

JESS   I thought this might be appreciated.

MAGGIE   Well I don't know what made you think that?

JESS   Just a wild guess!

              (*A beat.*)

MAGGIE	I'm on pain killers, you know that don't you?
JESS	Don't tell your doctor.
	(JESS *hands the beer to* MAGGIE, *both of them sit and look at each other, it is tempting to drink straight off.*)
MAGGIE	Go on then?
JESS	What?
MAGGIE	Down in one!
JESS	Me?
MAGGIE	Could you?
JESS	Could you?
MAGGIE	After three!
JESS	Do it!
MAGGIE	Yes?
JESS	Race you!
MAGGIE	You think you've got a chance?
JESS	Do you?
MAGGIE	I'm an expert!
JESS	So am I!
MAGGIE	Shall I call it?
JESS	And no cheating!
	(*A beat.*)

MAGGIE   One! Two! Three! Go!!

                  (*The two women start to drink. Music. Blackout.
                  Curtain.*)